From the author of *Simply Beautiful Beading...*

SIMPLY BEADED
BLISS

SIMPLY BEADED
BLISS

Adding Unique Elements to
Classic Beaded Jewelry, Gifts and Cards

HEIDI BOYD

NORTH LIGHT BOOKS
Cincinnati, Ohio
www.mycraftivity.com

12   11   10   09   08   5   4   3   2   1

Distributed in Canada by Fraser Direct
100 Armstrong Avenue
Georgetown, ON, Canada L7G 5S4
Tel: (905) 877-4411

Distributed in the U.K. and Europe by David & Charles
Brunel House, Newton Abbot, Devon, TQ12 4PU, England
Tel: (+44) 1626 323200, Fax: (+44) 1626 323319
E-mail: postmaster@davidandcharles.co.uk

Distributed in Australia by Capricorn Link
P.O. Box 704, S. Windsor, NSW 2756 Australia
Tel: (02) 4577-3555

Library of Congress Cataloging-in-Publication Data

Boyd, Heidi
   Simply beaded bliss : adding unique elements to classic beaded jewelry, gifts and cards / by Heidi Boyd. -- 1st ed.
     p. cm.
   Includes index.
   ISBN-13: 978-1-60061-095-0

   1. Beadwork. 2. Jewelry making. I. Title.
   TT860.B6878 2008
   745.58'2--dc22
                              2008017899

Metric Conversion Chart

to convert	to	multiply by
Inches	Centimeters	2.54
Centimeters	Inches	0.4
Feet	Centimeters	30.5
Centimeters	Feet	0.03
Yards	Meters	0.9
Meters	Yards	1.1
Sq. Inches	Sq. Centimeters	6.45
Sq. Centimeters	Sq. Inches	0.16
Sq. Feet	Sq. Meters	0.09
Sq. Meters	Sq. Feet	10.8
Sq. Yards	Sq. Meters	0.8
Sq. Meters	Sq. Yards	1.2
Pounds	Kilograms	0.45
Kilograms	Pounds	2.2
Ounces	Grams	28.3
Grams	Ounces	0.035

Editor: Jessica Gordon
Cover Designer: Marissa Bowers
Interior Designer: Dawn DeVries Sokol
Production Coordinator: Greg Nock
Photographers: Adam Henry, Alias Imaging, LLC, Ric Deliantoni
Stylist: Nora Martini

fw
F+W PUBLICATIONS, INC.

www.fwpublications.com

ABOUT THE AUTHOR

Heidi Boyd is the author of ten craft book titles with North Light, most notably the *Simply Beautiful* series. She crafts at the dining room table where she can keep an eye on the family and dash out the door for the next car pool. Her goal is to make sophisticated design approachable and easy for all. She has a fine art degree and got her start in professional crafting as a contributor to *Better Homes and Gardens* books and magazines. She and her family enjoy the natural beauty of Midcoast Maine. Check out her blog on www.mycraftivity.com.

DEDICATION

As you thumb through this book, you'll find mention of special friends and family members who have helped with individual projects. I really couldn't have pulled off this book without their help.

I'm blessed with a loving, tolerant family that doesn't complain when the kitchen counter is buried in art supplies that bear no resemblance to an edible meal, or when the dining room is an obstacle course of beads and half-finished projects for my latest book.

Special thanks to my two-year-old, Celia, who carefully "organizes" my beads without spilling a single one, but will dive under the table to find the ones I've dropped.

Jasper and Elliot, I appreciate you pitching in and watching your darling sister so I could make my deadline. To Elliot, a special thanks for cheering me on and telling me things actually looked good—that's a pretty big compliment from a junior high student!

To my husband, Jon, I want to say thank you for taking dozens of trips out to the garage to drill this, that and the other and for then figuring out what to make for dinner. For this and so much more, I love you dearly.

Thank you all for letting me enjoy this crazy career!

Acknowledgments

I owe a debt of gratitude to my editor, Jessica, for tediously working her way through boxes full of jewelry-making steps and transforming them into the beautiful photographs that appear throughout this book. It's magical to see project designs and instructions turn into a beautiful publication, which would not be possible without the talent and efforts of photo stylist, photographer and designer.

Contents

INTRODUCTION

It's time to expand your horizons and find new inspiration. In this book, you'll launch into brand-new mixed-media adventures in jewelry making. But don't worry—beads and stringing techniques are still at the heart of each project. What has changed is the wide range of UNEXPECTED supplies and methods that will inspire you to make your own beads, charms and pendants.

The first step in making mixed-media pieces is to stop shopping for all of your jewelry supplies in the jewelry aisle. Explore the hidden TREASURES hanging with the scrapbook supplies and the sewing notions. Check out toy and yarn shops. Grab your significant other and scour fishing tackle and hardware stores for potential jewelry-making supplies—your partner won't believe where you're taking him.

Be ready to break with tradition and use common materials in unconventional ways. Nail polish works beautifully on metal, so why not use it to make a pendant (see page 30)? Cut up old credit cards to make a playful bracelet (see page 64). Or try linking stainless steel washers to make an elegant bracelet or necklace (see page 40). Nail polish, credit cards and washers are just the beginning—this book is filled with clever twists. Once you realize how easy it is to CREATE wire beads and drill toys and found glass, you've become a mixed-media jewelry artist.

The days of working on little beading trays are over, so be prepared to make a mess. Spread your work out into the workshop and kitchen. New materials don't necessarily mean an investment in more tools. Toothpicks and straight pins are my favorite polymer clay tools. Common wax paper transforms any area into a protected work surface, perfect for shaping clay, applying protective coats and mixing cast resin.

I hope these projects tickle your sense of humor and that you have fun exploring new media and techniques. You'll come to expect second glances when you wear these BEAUTIFUL conversation pieces. Flip through the five chapters of different materials, then break out your stash of beads and tools and get ready to try something new. Don't be discouraged—it's really simple. As always, I've broken down everything into easy-to-follow steps. And the best part is that the new materials are readily available and inexpensive!

Enjoy, and wear your NEW JEWELRY with style!

—Heidi

TRADITIONAL JEWELRY SUPPLIES

Whatever style of jewelry you make, you'll always need a few standard materials, including findings, stringing wire or cording. If you're new to jewelry making, have no fear! This list will help you learn the ropes. Even if you're a pro, you might be surprised by what's available today, including an explosion of new earring findings in unique shapes and finishes.

General Findings

You'll need several basic findings, such as crimp beads and tubes, and head and eye pins.

Crimp beads and tubes are used to attach clasps to wire. Be sure to purchase crimps that will acco-modate a double thickness of your stringing wire. Select a gold, silver, black, copper or antique finish to match the stringing wire and clasp.

Head pins and eye pins are used to create dangles or link beaded elements. Head pins have a rounded flat end and eye pins have an open circle on one end. Head pins and eye pins come in different lengths in gold, silver, copper and antique metal finishes. Elaborate decorative head pins are often harder to manipulate. Fine sterling silver varieties are the easiest to shape.

Jump rings are small metal rings that can be opened and closed to link different jewelry components together. They are available in different sizes and metal finishes. The most expensive rings are sterling silver and gold-filled.

Split rings operate just like small key-chain rings: One end opens laterally, and the charm or chain link slips onto the ring. Split rings provide a more secure connection than jump rings. I've exclusively used the split rings sold with fishing tackle in the pieces throughout this book.

Clasps

Select a clasp that matches the scale and style of your beadwork. For instance, an ornate toggle clasp adds interest to a simply strand, whereas a small spring clasp better complements delicate beadwork.

Lobster clasps function like spring clasps, but each has an opening that allows it to hook onto a larger jump ring or leather loop.

Toggle clasps come in many different variations. Each piece is crimped onto a strand end. To fasten, fit the toggle completely through the O-ring.

Earring Findings

Earrings are some of the quickest jewelry projects to make. Whip up a quick pair by linking simple dangles to the findings of your choice or by wire wrapping beads to a hoop.

French earwires have a simple fishhook shape that passes through the ear. The French earwires I've used in my designs are often larger than the traditional variety.

Hoop earrings are great for wire wrapping with beads or for suspending dangles from the center loop.

colored wire

32-gauge wire

heavy-gauge wire

Wire and Chain

Wire and chain are often the foundation of beaded jewelry. A higher gauge indicates thinner wire or chain, while a lower gauge signals thicker wire or chain.

32-gauge wire is very thin and easily threads through small seed beads. It's usually available in both gold and silver finishes.

Both **silver-plated and sterling silver wire** are good choices for jewelry. Sterling silver is the more expensive choice, but it's longer lasting because it can always be polished to restore its sheen. Wire comes in a multitude of thicknesses and colored finishes, so be careful to select the size indicated for each project.

Cabled stringing wire is made up of multiple fine wires encased in a protective nylon coating. It comes in a range of thicknesses and colors. The strength and flexibility of the wire is determined by the number of core wires, from 7 through 49. Use the most flexible rating for projects where the wire will be bent and doubled. Reserve more expensive gold- and silver-plated stringing wires for pieces where the wire is visible. Use less expensive wires for simple lightweight beading.

cabled stringing wire

Link chain is sold in a variety of thicknesses, from very fine chain to heavy round links. It is available in a wide variety of metal contents, including plated and solid sterling. All chain can be easily broken into smaller lengths by simply cutting open a single link with wire cutters. Explore the amazing range of new link shapes and faux antique finishes.

Leather and faux suede cord are sold by the yard in jewelry and fabric stores and by packaged lengths in craft stores.

Clear elastic cording makes stringing larger beads a breeze. For a more secure connection, 1mm heavyweight elastic is substantial enough to be crimped.

NONTRADITIONAL JEWELRY SUPPLIES

This list will help guide your search for materials outside of the jewelry aisle. These nontraditional items are commonly used for many crafts and hobbies, from sewing to fishing. They should be easy to find—if you're lucky, they might already be lurking in your sewing, tool or fishing tackle box!

Fabric and Notions

Most large craft chains carry these soft craft items, but if you visit local specialty stores, you'll be treated to a unique selection of unusual buttons and sequins.

Wool roving is cleaned and dyed brushed wool that's ready for spinning or felting. It's most commonly available where knitting, spinning and weaving supplies are sold. A small amount of roving makes quite a few beads. For jewelry making, it's ideal to buy small quantities in a variety of colors.

Snaps are available in a few different sizes and come secured to a cardboard hanger. They're inexpensive, so if you're planning to link them together, grab an extra sheet.

Buttons work very well as jewelry components. Be on the lookout for buttons—if you're lucky you'll stumble across an old jar filled to the brim. I can easily spend a half an hour contemplating racks of buttons at the fabric store.

Sequins have traditionally been used to decorate sewing projects, but the lightweight iridescent embellishments are now sold in the general craft and scrapbooking aisles as well. It's amazing how many different colors and shapes come in a single variety package.

Home Improvement and Hobby

I never have a problem persuading my husband to join me on shopping trips to fishing tackle and hardware stores. It's a welcome change from my endless trips to craft stores.

Fishing tackle is readily available where I live in Maine. I'm lucky to have L.L.Bean right down the road—it's actually closer than the grocery store. They have a terrific selection of fishing tackle. I was also able to pick up items at the Kittery Trading Post. If you can't find what you need locally, try Cabela's catalog. When you're shopping for tackle, keep the scale of your work in mind and also try to select metals that will wear well. Brass and stainless steel are safe choices. Examine the lures to make sure the hooks can be easily removed, and watch for sharp edges.
Make sure you stock up on split rings. The fishing tackle variety are super strong and make great connectors.

Washers make surprisingly good jewelry components. I like to pour through open-stock hardware bins to find the right weight and size washers for my work. It's also convenient to count out the quantity you need without being tied into a pre-packaged number. Be sure you stick to the stainless steel variety—they're slightly more expensive, but you wouldn't want your creation to rust with age and wear.

Plastics

If you thought making jewelry with plastic was a job for commercial manufacturing, you're wrong. It's so easy to explore and enjoy the versatility of this medium at home.

Resin is a liquid polymer that sets into clear, shiny plastic. There are many different cast-resin solutions on the market. I use Envirotex, which mixes equal parts of cast and resin together. Other varieties use a catalyst to trigger the chemical reaction. Whichever type you select, be sure to follow the safety precautions. If you want to adapt the project for children, substitute layers of Glossy Accents.

Micro beads, or miniature beads, are tiny balls without holes. They're sold in different color mixes, either loose or mixed into a glue compound called Liquid Beadz.

Polymer clay is an easy-to-use clay-like compound that is cured by baking it in a conventional oven (no kiln required). The clay is available in a whole host of colors.

Shrink art sheets are pieces of plastic that shrink dramatically when baked in a conventional oven. The sheets used in this book are specially manufactured to run through an inkjet printer. Traditional shrink art sheets are available in black, white and clear. They can be stamped or colored with permanent markers and colored pencils.

Any **miniature toy** can become a piece of jewelry. Take a second look at clutter and trinkets before tossing them in the garbage. If they don't already have a stringing hole, you can most likely drill one.

Scrapbook Embellishments

Paper comes in a vast array of colors, patterns and textures. As a rule, use thin paper for beads and cardstock to back paper charms and brooches.

Eyelets frame a punched hole. The two parts are threaded through either side of the paper and a setter tool locks them together. They're available in a myriad of different colors, sizes and finishes.

Bookplates are manufatured to frame words on scrapbook pages. Placing bookplates back-to-back creates a great setting for polymer clay.

Look for different shapes, sizes, colors and metal finishes.

TYPES OF BEADS

E beads

To say there is a wide variety of beads on the market is a vast understatement. In this book, the mixed-media beads and charms often become the centerpiece of the design. They can't stand alone, and the success of the final creation is dependent on how well they're integrated with surrounding beads. Stock up on seed and E beads—they're inexpensive, they make great fillers and they're used in almost every project. Wood beads are a perfect complement to resin and felt beads; crystal beads add sparkle to any project; and natural stone beads create the ideal framework for Chinese and silver charms. Following are brief descriptions of some of the beads used in this book.

Seed beads are tiny, inexpensive beads available in a wide range of colors and finishes, including metallic. Some beads are clear with a colored inside lining. They come in lots of different sizes, and the size of their openings also varies. Make sure you select beads that work with the specified stringing materials. Traditional seed beads are slightly irregular with some holes larger than others. If consistency is important to your design, look for Delica seed beads that are uniform in shape and size.

SIZE CHART

Round beads are easy to measure on a millimeter size chart and are usually packaged with the size printed on the package label or on the container in the bead store. You'll find many of the beads in this book aren't sized because they come from mixed-variety bags or don't have a uniform shape.

Bead Chart

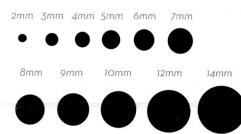

2mm 3mm 4mm 5mm 6mm 7mm

8mm 9mm 10mm 12mm 14mm

E beads are slightly larger than seed beads and also come in a myriad of colors and sizes. E beads are especially useful for framing and spacing other beads. Magatama beads have the same size opening as E beads, but they're semi-teardrop-shaped.

Bugle beads are small tubes that come in different lengths and colors. Their openings are close in size to those of seed beads.

Czech glass beads get their unique shapes by being pressed into molds. Flowers and leaves are the most common varieties. The advantage of selecting Czech beads is that you can purchase multiples of the same size.

Crystal beads are intricately faceted to reflect light and add sparkle to any beaded piece. They come in round, cube and bicone shapes. The prices of these beads vary dramatically; the more expensive Austrian varieties such as Swarovski lead crystal are clearer and more reflective than the more economical generic crystal beads.

Freshwater pearls range in size from the smallest rice pearl to an elongated 13mm-long tube shape. The pearls are usually coated with an iridescent colored finish that highlights their inherent irregularities.

Glass pearls are glass beads covered with a pearlescent coating. They are an affordable and effective costume jewelry alternative to natural pearls.

plastic game pieces

pink-lined
clear plastic
beads

rolled
paper
beads

seed beads

freshwater and
glass pearls

*In mustard dish, clockwise
from left: semiprecious
stone beads in turquoise,
coral, jade and carnelian;
resin and shell beads;
garnet stone chips;
Chinese charms.*

glass beads

plastic beads

semiprecious
rounds

Semiprecious stone rounds, beads and chips
are formed from natural and semiprecious stones.
They're made from a wide variety of stones, from
jasper to jade. They're cut and polished into smooth
round, faceted or small chip beads with center-drilled
holes. The irregularity of the natural stone makes
each of these beads unique.

Spacer beads come in a variety of metal finishes,
shapes and sizes. Keep a selection on hand, as their
neutral color makes them the perfect accompaniment
to almost all bead types.

*In green dish (at top), clockwise from left:
Swarovski crystals, wooden beads, resin beads,
sea glass, sterling silver charms*

Plastic beads and playing pieces are lightweight
beads that can be found in children's craft and toy
boxes—but they make perfect complements to
whimsical beading projects.

Coral and shell beads are natural elements cut into
all different sizes and shapes. Their natural sheen and
color add interest and rich texture to your beadwork.

THE BASICS

Making mixed-media jewelry is the perfect excuse to stock up on some groovy new gadgets. Most of these items have many uses and will come in handy in all kinds of crafting pursuits. The right tool for the job is critical to the ease and success of your work.

Round-nose pliers have two smooth, round tapered pincers that facilitate shaping wire into coils or loops.

Chain-nose or needle-nose pliers are commonly used in wire jewelry projects. They're perfect for holding jewelry while wire ends get wrapped.

Flush or wire cutters are essential for trimming wire and chain links. Save your scissors—it's safer and easier to make a quick clip with wire cutters than to exert too much pressure with scissors blades.

Scissors with small sharp points that fit easily in tight places are a must-have for any crafter. Any good quality scissors will work, but my scissors of choice are Fiskars Softouch Micro-Tip. The built-in spring is activated by a light touch on the hand grips. The center locking mechanism and plastic sleeve make them portable and easy to stow.

Crimping pliers have specialized jaws for squeezing a crimp tube flat. If you're flattening only a crimp bead or a small crimp, you may be able to substitute a pair of chain-nose pliers. It takes a little practice to get comfortable positioning the crimping tube in the appropriate grooves to make a double crimp, but the resulting connection is very sturdy.

Electric drills are a must-have for many mixed-media jewelry projects. Most of the time, the directions will ask you to drill through rubber and lightweight plastics. The exception is drilling through sea glass. For these pieces, we used my husband's conventional full-sized drill outfitted with a $\frac{1}{16}$" (2mm) bit. Be sure to follow all safety precautions, including wearing protective eyewear. When necessary, brace or clamp the item you're drilling to protect your fingers.

Clockwise from bottom left: chain-nose pliers, paper punch, instant setter, wire cutters, scissors, crimping pliers, round-nose pliers, shank cutters, electric drill on top of paper trimmer

Clear stamps can be used interchangeably with **acrylic blocks**. To use these stamps, simply press the desired image onto an acrylic block, ink it and stamp it. This setup is perfect for jewelry work because you can see exactly where to place the stamp and watch it in action.

Instant setters make setting eyelets a breeze. First use the punch attachment to make the hole. Thread the eyelet through the punched hole. Swap out the punch for the setter and simply push the setter into the eyelet. Presto, you've got a perfectly set eyelet. If you've ever struggled with the separate pieces and had to hammer the eyelet in place, you'll love this alternative.

Paper trimmers make cutting straight edges a breeze. Just line the paper sheet up along the grid lines and drag the blade down the slot for a quick, easy cut. A 12" (30cm) size paper cutter is small enough to fit in the chaos of my work table, and the straightforward blade is easy to operate and replace.

Shank cutters are slick little tools. I picked mine up on a whim when I was button shopping. I was amazed how effortlessly it sheared the shanks off plastic buttons. If you love buttons and want to make jewelry with them, this is a good tool to have on hand.

Paintbrushes are used mainly to apply clear coats of hardener, glue and acrylic tints. You can get by with any brush small enough to fit into tiny crevices and withstand multiple washings. Very inexpensive brushes tend to break apart and lose bristles, so look for a moderately priced brush and make sure you rinse it immediately after every use.

METAL AND
CHAIN

I'll begin the heavy metal chapter with a confession: I do not enjoy metal-smithing. I tried unsuccessfully to take a class on the subject, and I quickly discovered that my idea of creative expression is not trying to bash a piece of metal into a rounded shape against an anvil. I've since made my peace with metal and found simple ways to integrate it into my designs. If I can control it with my fingertips and pliers, it's included in this chapter. If it requires full-body strength, you'll have to sign yourself up for a metalworking class.

Wire is the simplest way to introduce metalwork into your beading. It's lightweight, and you can quickly and easily manipulate it with chain-nose pliers. It comes in a myriad of gauges and finishes, making it easy to find the perfect match for any design. In this chapter, you'll find wire used in lots of different ways. In the *Wrapped Pearl Earrings* (see page 26), it's used as a decorative element. In the *Wrapped Wire Bead Necklace* (see page 34), the wire becomes the bead. The heaviest gauge wire is used to create a sculptural earring tree (see page 44).

Before I lose my chain of thought, let's contemplate the merits of links. They also come in a wide assortment of finishes and weights. Recently, I've seen a surge of chain link in the jewelry market. Both the *Cascade Necklace* (see page 28) and the *Chain Link Chandelier Earrings* (see page 22) use lightweight products that are not only easy to work with but create jewelry that's comfortable to wear.

Both hardware and fishing tackle departments stock ready-to-use jewelry products—they just don't realize it. Check out the *Hardware Bracelet* (see page 40) and the *Fishing Tackle Bracelet* (see page 38) to see unconventional metal components transformed into attractive wearable jewelry. These nifty creations will start up all kinds of interesting conversations.

WIRED HOOPS

Materials

- 2 hoops
  (Blue Moon Beads)
- red triangle beads
  (Blue Moon Beads)
- 8 clear foil E beads
- 8 red bicone beads
- 2 14" (36cm) lengths
  of 32-gauge
  beading wire
- 2 head pins

Tools: wire cutters,
round-nose pliers

*Finished dangle length:
2" (5cm)*

Transform plain hoop forms into sparkly beaded earrings with this easy wrapping technique. Ultra-fine wire blends well against the hoop form and lets the beads shine. This project hinges on a simple equation: more wraps = more beads = more sparkle!

Periwinkle Wired Hoops

This technique is easily adaptable to all hoop sizes and bead colors. Simply increase the wire length and the number of beads for larger hoops and decrease both for smaller hoops.

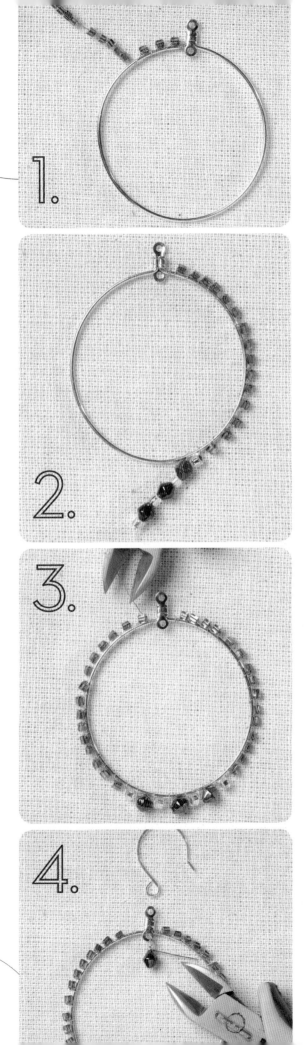

ONE: Begin to wrap beads

Tightly wrap 1 end of the beading wire around the top of the hoop 3 or 4 times. String 15 red triangle beads onto the wire. Slide the first bead right up against the wrapped wire end on the top of the hoop. Bring the wire under and through the hoop. Position the second bead alongside the first and wrap the wire under and through the hoop again, securing the beads to the hoop. Continue working in this fashion until all 15 beads are secured to the hoop.

TWO: Continue wrapping beads

Alternating between E beads and bicones, string 7 beads onto the wire, ending with an E bead. Slide the first E bead up against the last triangle bead, and bring the wire under and through the hoop to wrap the bead to the hoop. Repeat the process to individually wrap each of the strung beads in place.

THREE: Finish wrapping beads to hoop

String 15 more red triangle beads onto the wire and wrap them in place, ending at the top of the hoop. Tightly wrap the wire end around the hoop 3 or 4 times. Trim the excess wire with wire cutters.

FOUR: Add bead dangle

String a red bicone bead onto a head pin. Create a wrapped loop above the bead with round-nose pliers and hook it onto the ring at the top of the hoop. (See Techniques, page 140, for instructions on making a wrapped loop.) Wrap the head pin end under the shaped loop and then trim the end. Hook the earring finding through the top of the finished hoop earring. Repeat the process to create the second earring.

CHAIN LINK CHANDELIER EARRINGS

Materials

* 2 3" (8cm) lengths of small link chain (Blue Moon Beads)
* 2 wooden beads
* 6 Apple resin beads (Blue Moon Beads)
* 4 teardop shell beads (Blue Moon Beads)
* 4 brown foil E beads
* 4 brown foil seed beads
* 2 5" (13cm) lengths of 22-gauge silver-plated wire (Beadalon)
* 2 earring findings
* 2 eye pins
* 4 jump rings

Tools: round-nose pliers, chain-nose pliers, wire cutters

Finished dangle length: 2" (5cm)

This earring features an unlikely mix of natural shell, wooden, glass and resin beads strung horizontally onto thin wire. The wire ends hook onto a small length of chain to make unique triangular drop earrings.

ONE: Link wire to chain

Use round-nose pliers to turn a loop in 1 end of the wire, link the end of the chain into the loop and wrap the loop closed. Trim the wire end with wire cutters. (See Techniques, page 140, for instructions on making a wrapped loop.)

TWO: String beads onto wire

Slide each teardrop onto a jump ring, and use pliers to tightly close the rings. (See Techniques, page 141, for instructions on opening and closing a jump ring.) String beads onto the wire in the following sequence: seed bead, E bead, green resin bead, teardrop, resin bead, teardrop, resin bead, E bead, seed bead.

THREE: Secure beaded wire to chain

Shape the free end of the wire into a loop, slide it through the free end of the chain, and then wrap the loop closed. Trim away the excess wire with wire cutters.

FOUR: Finish earring

Hook the eye pin into the center link of the chain. Thread a wooden bead onto the eye pin and then make a wrapped loop above the bead. Trim away the excess wire. Hook an earring finding to the top of the loop. Repeat to make the second earring.

23

CHAIN LINK TASSEL EARRINGS

Materials

* 10 1¼" (3cm) lengths of small link chain (Blue Moon Beads)
* 2 blue resin beads (Blue Moon Beads)
* 2 round wooden beads
* 2 small silver bead caps
* 2 small flower connectors
* 2 3" (8cm) lengths of 22-gauge silver-plated wire (Beadalon)
* 2 hook earring findings
* 4 3mm silver jump rings

Tools: round-nose pliers, wire cutters

Finished dangle length: 2½" (6cm)

For a new twist on fiber tassels, hook multiple lightweight lengths of chain together with an eye pin to make a lightweight metal tassel. The tassel is topped with an interesting mixture of wood, resin and shell beads. This design can be easily adapted by using chain with a different finish or by choosing chain made with smaller or larger links. If you change the chain, be sure to switch up the beads to match.

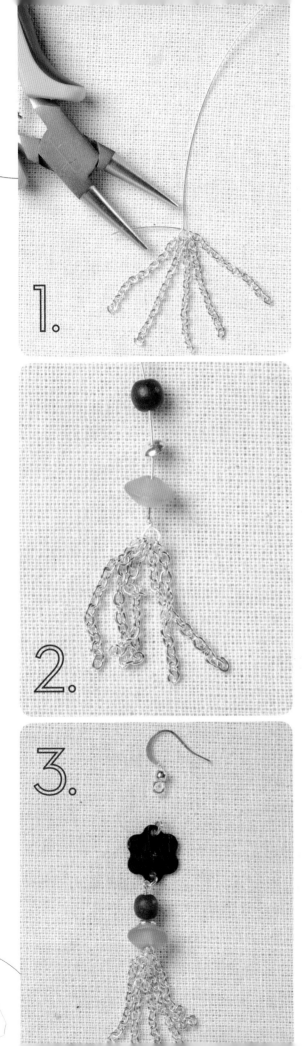

ONE: Link chain sections to wire loop

Use the center of the round-nose pliers to create a slightly larger than usual loop in 1 end of the wire. (See Techniques, page 140, for instructions on turning a loop.) Hook the first link of each of the 5 chain sections onto the wire loop. Wrap the loop closed. (See Techniques, page 140, for instructions on creating a wrapped loop.)

TWO: String beads onto wire

String the following sequence of beads onto the open wire end: blue resin bead, bead cap, wooden bead.

THREE: Finish earring

Shape the wire end into a smaller regular-sized loop, and then wrap the wire around the base of the loop and trim the end. Link the tassel to a flower-shaped connector with a jump ring. (See Techniques, page 141, for instructions on opening and closing a jump ring.) Link the flower connector to an earring finding with a second jump ring. Repeat to make the second earring.

WRAPPED PEARL EARRINGS

Materials

* 2 top-drilled freshwater pearls
* 2 small freshwater pearls
* 2 10mm round teal Swarovski crystal beads
* 24-gauge silver-plated wire (Beadalon)
* 2 lightweight silver head pins
* 2 large split rings
* earring findings (Blue Moon Beads)
* Beadfix jewelry glue (Beadalon)

Tools: round-nose pliers, wire cutters, chain-nose pliers

Finished dangle length: 1¹/₂" (4cm)

This wrapping technique is an easy way to give handmade jewelry a professional appearance. The key is to locate top-drilled pearls and stones—it's almost impossible to wrap center-drilled beads. Look for high-quality sterling or sterling-plated wire that will wrap easily and complement your beads. For these earrings, I've combined the wrapped beads with small freshwater pearls, crystals and large jump rings.

Wrapped Pearl Necklace

This necklace features all of the techniques used in the earrings. Switch to heavier 22-gauge wire to balance the weight of the stone. String all the bead elements onto silver-plated stringing wire, then finish the necklace by hanging a small freshwater pearl dangle from one side of the clasp.

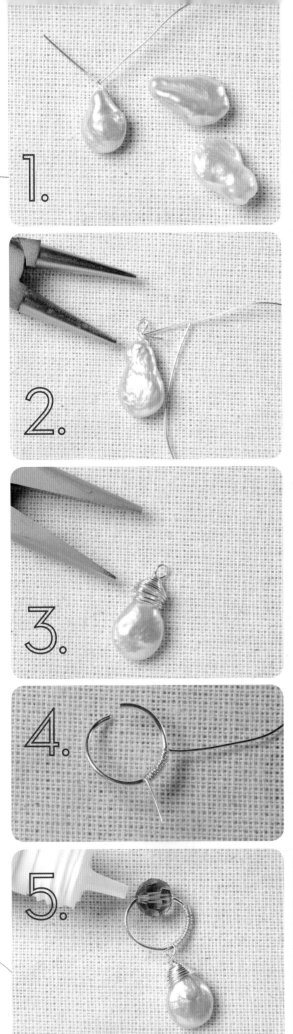

ONE: Twist wires on top of pearl
String the wire end through the pearl, pulling through 1" (3cm) of wire. Bring the wires up to the top of the pearl and twist them together once.

TWO: Create loop
Use round-nose pliers to turn a loop in the short end of the wire. Wrap the other end of the wire around the base of the loop, using chain-nose pliers to keep the wrap even, if necessary. (See Techniques, page 140, for instructions on creating a wrapped loop.)

THREE: Create wire wrap
Continue wrapping the wire until the bead hole is completely concealed. Use chain-nose pliers to make fine adjustments in the wrapped wire. Trim the end and apply a dot of jewelry glue to the wire end to help hold it in place.

FOUR: Wire wrap jump ring
Laterally open a jump ring (see Techniques, page 141, for instructions on opening and closing a jump ring) and begin wrapping 1 end of a 5" (13cm) length of 24-gauge wire around the jump ring. Continue wrapping for ¼" (1cm), then trim the wire. Use chain-nose pliers to compress the wrapped wires.

FIVE: Secure crystal bead
String a wire-wrapped pearl onto the jump ring. Place the crystal bead onto 1 end of the jump ring, then press the other end of the jump ring into the other side of the crystal. Inserting the ends into the ring will distort the jump ring, so use chain-nose pliers to readjust it. Insert glue into the crystal bead opening to help anchor the ring to the bead.

SIX: Finish earring with pearl dangle
String a small freshwater pearl onto a head pin. Make a wrapped loop above the bead, then trim the wire and thread it onto an earring finding. Loop the earring finding around the wire-wrapped jump ring. Repeat to make a second earring.

CASCADE NECKLACE

Materials

* silver metal oval (Blue Moon Beads)
* generous assortment of purple and green glass beads
* 4mm and 6mm olivine and purple bicone Swarovski crystals
* small silver metal bead caps (Blue Moon Beads)
* 2¹/₂" (6cm) of silver metal link chain (Blue Moon)
* 2 oval split rings (Beadalon)
* lightweight silver metal head pins (Blue Moon)
* lightweight silver metal eye pins (Blue Moon)
* 36" (91cm) purple silk cord (Beadin' Path)

Tools: round-nose pliers, chain-nose pliers, wire cutters

Finished dangle length, including oval ring: 4" (10cm)

Like a rippling waterfall, this beaded pendant catches the light and changes with your every movement. The glass and crystal beads are connected with thin head pins and chain, creating a surprisingly lightweight finished pendant that's comfortable to wear. You could easily downsize this design to make cascading earrings.

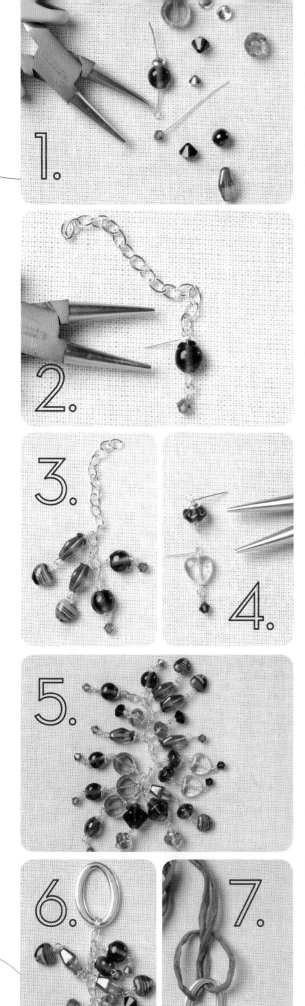

ONE: Make 2-bead dangles

String a 4mm bicone bead onto a head pin, and create a wrapped loop above the bead. (See Techniques, page 140, for instructions on making a wrapped loop.) Trim the wire end with wire cutters. String the larger bead onto an eye pin, top it with a small bead cap and shape the end into a loop, but don't wrap it yet.

TWO: Link dangle to chain

Hook the smaller bead onto the bottom of the beaded eye pin. Hook the top of the shaped eye pin onto the last link of the chain, then finish wrapping the loop and trim the wire end. Repeat to add a second 2-bead dangle to the next link up in the chain.

THREE: Continue linking dangles

Make another pair of 2-bead dangles, adding each individual dangle to a chain link. My example features small heart beads and long diamond-shaped glass beads. Any bead combinations will work, just remember to increase both the overall length of the dangles and the size of the top beads as you make your way up the chain. Make 3 more pairs of 2-bead dangles and attach them to the chain.

FOUR: Make 3-bead dangles

String a small bicone bead onto a head pin and create a wrapped loop above the bead. String a large heart bead onto an eye pin and create a wrapped loop above that bead as well. String a purple glass bead and a bead cap onto a second eye pin and turn a loop above the beads, but don't wrap the loop until the dangle is connected to the chain. Hook the bicone to the bottom of the heart and hook the heart to the bottom of the purple glass bead. Repeat to make a matching dangle for the next chain link.

FIVE: Finish cascade dangle

Make 6 more 3-bead dangles and add them to the chain, placing 2 dangles on the last 2 links of the chain.

SIX: Connect cascade dangle to oval ring

Use a pair of oval jump rings to connect the top link of the finished dangle to the metal oval ring. (See Techniques, page 141, for instructions on opening and closing jump rings.)

SEVEN: Knot silk cord to oval ring

Fold the silk cord in half and pass the center of the fold through the metal oval ring. Draw both cord ends through the center loop and pull them up. Tie the ends of the cord together in a loose overhand knot before slipping it over your head.

29

POLISHED PENDANT

Materials

* round metal disks (Blue Moon Beads)
* green, yellow, orange and pink nail polish
* lime green seed beads
* orange Magatama beads (Beadalon)
* glass bead
* 16" (41cm) stringing wire (Beadalon)
* crimp beads
* head pin
* jump ring
* toothpicks
* wax paper or index card

Tools: crimping pliers, wire cutters, chain-nose and round-nose pliers

Finished necklace length: 15½" (39cm)

If you've ever been entranced by the shimmer of nail polish, this is the perfect way to explore it as an artistic medium. It's so easy to use—just shake the bottle and use the built-in brush to apply it directly to a blank metal disk. The results are amazing—it looks just like real enamel. Next time your friends are about to spend time on their nails, slip them a couple of blank disks and their handiwork is guaranteed to last longer than any manicure!

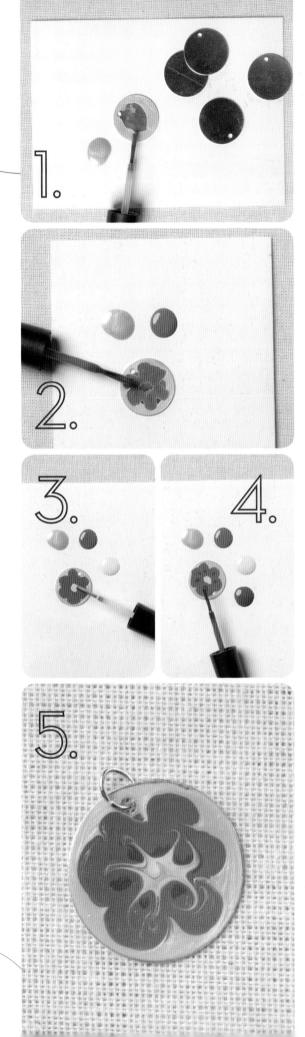

ONE: Apply green polish to disk

Working on top of wax paper or an index card, apply a ring of green polish around the outside of the disk. Allow it to dry.

TWO: Apply orange polish

Apply 6 generous dollops of orange polish in a circle to create flower petals.

THREE: Add yellow polish

Drop a spot of yellow nail polish in the center of the petals. Work quickly from here—don't let the yellow polish dry.

FOUR: Add pink polish

Add a small dot of pink polish to the inside edge of each petal. Use a toothpick to drag the yellow out from the center to create decorative swirls.

FIVE: Slide pendant onto jump ring

Let the polish pendant dry overnight. Thread a jump ring onto the finished pendant.

SIX: String pendant onto necklace

Crimp 1 part of the clasp to 1 end of the stringing wire. (See Techniques, page 139, for instructions on securing a clasp with a crimp tube.) String on 1 orange Magatama bead, then bead the length of the wire with lime green seed beads, stopping halfway to add the pendant.

SEVEN: Finish necklace

Continue beading until the beaded length equals 15" (38cm). Thread the glass bead onto a head pin, and shape the wire end into a wrapped loop. (See Techniques, page 140, for instructions on making a wrapped loop.) String on an orange Magatama bead, the glass bead dangle and a second orange Magatama bead. Crimp the other part of the clasp to the wire end, and trim the wire end with wire cutters.

TIP

Nail polish doesn't just come in pinks and reds anymore—you'll be amazed not only by the color selection but by the varieties of glitter, sparkles and shimmers that are embedded in the paints.

∼ Pink and Purple Polished Pendant and Earrings

If you don't want to mess with drops of nail polish, here's the easiest solution: Apply two different colors of paint and simply swirl them together with the end of a toothpick.

Polished Earrings

Materials

* 4 small metal disks
* 2 orange glass Magatama beads (Beadalon)
* fishhook earring findings
* 1 3mm silver-plated jump ring
* 1 4mm silver-plated oval jump ring

Tools: round-nose pliers

In the mood to paint, not bead? Set up four disks side by side and paint them assembly-line style. In minutes, you'll create matching two-sided earrings.

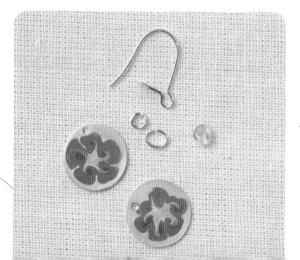

Create 4 miniature flower disks, 2 for each earring. Place each pair back to back and secure them together with a round jump ring. (See Techniques, page 141, for instructions on opening and closing a jump ring.) Thread the fishhook finding through the jump ring, adding a single bead to the finding at the same time. Repeat the process to make a second earring.

WRAPPED WIRE BEAD NECKLACE

Materials

* 4" (10cm) sections of 24-gauge wire in icy silver, icy copper, black and gold (Toner Plastics)
* seed beads in silver, matte silver, gold and copper
* short twisted silver bugle beads
* 2 black E beads
* 2 18" (46cm) strands of .018" (5mm) stringing wire (Beadalon)
* O-ring and toggle clasp (Blue Moon Beads)
* no. 3 crimp tubes
* heavyweight head pins

Tools: round-nose pliers, wire cutters, crimping pliers

Finished length: 17" (43cm)

Get all wound up with wire when you create this project. Wrapping simple wire into cool beads will make you take a second look at wire's jewelry-making potential. By simply coiling wire then switching directions and wrapping it some more, you will start to form a bead. Add a second wire length in a different color to make the bead even more interesting. Set your beautiful wire beads among a random mix of metallic seed beads.

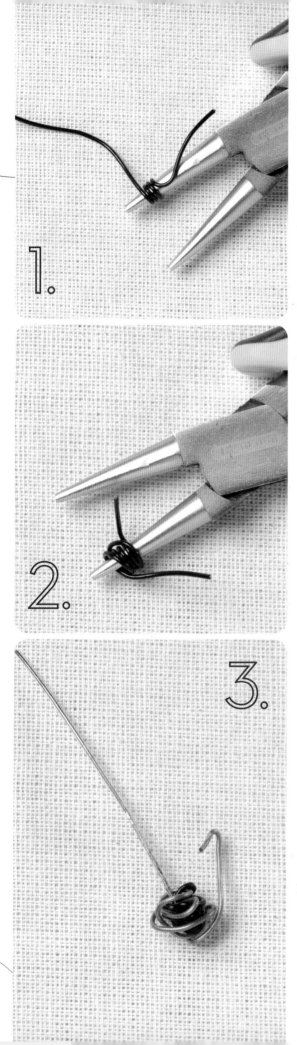

ONE: Coil black wire

Wrap the end of the black wire around 1 pincer of the round-nose pliers 3 times to make a coil.

TWO: Coil black wire into bead core

With the first coil still in place on the pliers, coil the wire 3 more times at a vertical angle over the first coil. Trim the wire ends, fold them down and poke them into the coils.

THREE: Wrap gold wire around bead core

Slide the bead core off the pliers and onto a heavyweight head pin. Hook 1 end of a gold wire section into the black wire and begin wrapping the gold wire around the black wire core. Wrap it up, down, around and side to side. Trim the wire end, fold it down and poke it into the black wire.

FOUR: Add copper wire

Wrap a length of copper wire around the bead in different directions. Trim the end, and then poke the wire down into the wrapped wire.

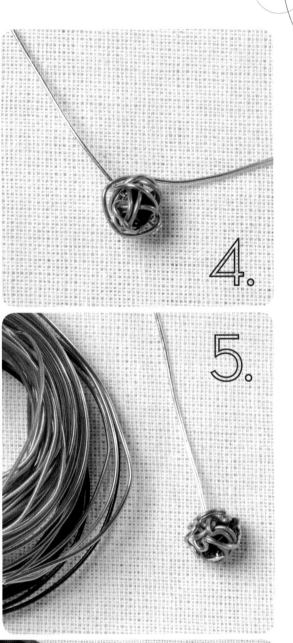

FIVE: Finish bead

Using round-nose pliers, grab 1 of the outer metallic wires and gently twist it against the surface of the bead. Repeat to bend all the outer wires. This process will transform the appearance of the straight wire wrapping into round, twisted loops. It also tightens the surface of the bead. Leave the finished bead on the head pin until you're ready to thread it onto the stringing wire to help you find the opening. You'll need 9 wire beads to make the 2-strand necklace.

SIX: String first strand

Tape 1 end of an 18" (46cm) length of stringing wire, and then string it with 3³/₄" (10cm) of random seed and twisted bugle beads. Transfer a wire bead to the wire from a head pin. String another 2¹/₂" (6cm) of random beads and add another wire bead. Repeat this sequence 2 more times to string a total of 4 wire beads, ending with 3¹/₂" (9cm) of seed and bugle beads.

7.

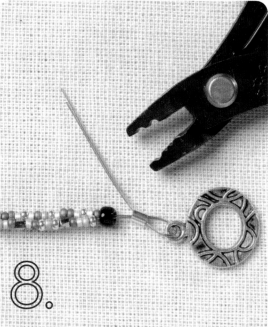

8.

SEVEN: String second strand

Tape the end of the second wire, and string 2¹/2" (6cm) of random beads, then transfer a wire bead from a head pin to the beaded strand. String 2¹/2" (6cm) of beads and add another wire bead. Repeat this sequence 3 more times for a total of 5 wire beads. End with 2" (5cm) of beads. The spacing of beads in steps 6 and 7 staggers the wire beads so that when the strands are joined, the beads are evenly distributed

EIGHT: Finish necklace

Bring the ends of the 2 strands together and string them both through an E bead, crimp tube, clasp and back through the crimp. Pull the strands tight. Crimp the tube twice and trim the end of the wire. (See Techniques, page 139, for instructions on securing a clasp with a crimp tube.) Repeat with the bar end of the toggle clasp at the other end of the necklace.

Wrapped Wire Bead Earrings ~~~~~

Make two identical beads as you did for the neck-lace (see steps 1 through 5). Don't slide each bead off its head pin when you've finished. Instead, create a wrapped loop above the bead and hook the result-ing dangle onto an earring finding. (See Techniques, page 140, for instructions on making a wrapped loop.) Repeat to make a second earring.

FISHING TACKLE BRACELET

Materials

* 2 round Millefiori glass beads
* 1 square Millefiori glass bead
* turquoise seed beads
* a variety of different shaped glass beads in turquoise, blue and green
* 3 brass 3-way swivels (sold with fishing tackle)
* gold fish-shaped lure (sold with fishing tackle)
* 6 3½" (9cm) lengths .015" (4mm) gold stringing wire (Beadalon)
* 11 gold crimp beads
* 3 gold head pins
* lobster clasp
* 6mm gold split ring

Tools: wire cutters and crimping pliers, round-nose pliers

Finished length: 7½" (19cm)

I have a faint memory of making a snap-swivel-and-seed bead bracelet when I was a teenager, and I wanted to update the concept for this book. My father-in-law, expert fisherman Mark Boyd, patiently navigated me around the fishing departments at L.L.Bean and Kittery Trading Post, where I found a treasure trove of potential jewelry-making supplies, including the brass three-way swivels and fish-shaped lures featured in this design (as well as the split rings in the *It's-a-Snap Bracelet* [see page 126]).

Fishing Tackle Necklace

Link beaded strands using three-way swivels, and attach dangles to some of the free holes to make a fishing tackle necklace.

ONE: Crimp wires to swivel rings

Crimp a 3½" (9cm) length of stringing wire to 2 of the 3 brass rings on 1 swivel. (See Techniques, page 139, for instructions on securing wire with crimps.)

TWO: String on beads

String each wire with 1½" (4cm) of random glass and seed beads. Crimp each end to a ring on a second swivel. Cut the ends of the wire with wire cutters.

THREE: Add dangle to free swivel ring

String a head pin with a seed bead and a round Millefiori bead, and make a loop above the bead with round-nose pliers. (See Techniques, page 140, for instructions on turning and wrapping loops.) Hook the loop onto the third ring on the second swivel, wrap the end and trim the wire.

FOUR: Begin to bead second section

Crimp another stringing wire to the ring with the dangle. String this wire with 1½" (4cm) of random beads. Crimp the other end of this wire to a ring on a third swivel. Hook a second seed bead and Millefiori bead dangle onto the same ring.

FIVE: Attach clasp

Crimp 2 more wires to the third swivel. Bead the wires and crimp them to a fourth swivel. Use a split ring to attach the lobster clasp to the last swivel ring. The clasp will hook onto the empty ring on the first swivel.

SIX: Separate fish from lure

Use round-nose pliers and wire cutters to carefully cut the fish-hook (it's sharp!) and connector from the lure.

SEVEN: Add final dangles

String the last head pin with a seed bead and a square Millefiori bead, shape the end and hook it through the bottom of the swivel ring before wrapping and trimming the wire end. String the last wire through the top of the fishing lure and then pass the ends in opposite directions through a crimp bead. Use chain-nose pliers to smash the crimp bead flat, securing the fish charm.

HARDWARE BRACELET

Materials

* stainless steel washers
* 4mm silver beads
* 4mm glass cat eye beads (Blue Moon Beads)
* brown slide-cut glass cat eye beads (Blue Moon Beads)
* 5 3½" (9cm) lengths of .024" (6mm) 19-strand stringing wire (Beadalon)
* O-ring and toggle clasp (Blue Moon Beads)
* no. 2 silver-plated crimp tubes (Beadalon)

Tools: crimping pliers, wire cutters

Finished length: 7¼" (18cm)

Gentlemen, lock up your toolboxes. Nothing is safe with a crafty lady in the house. Transform plain stainless steel washers from your local hardware store into fabulous jewelry with a simple link-and-crimp technique. It's important to find substantial beads to offset the combined weight of the heavy stringing wire and the stainless steel washers. The size, shape and translucency of these smoky topaz side-cut glass numbers from Blue Moon work beautifully.

Hardware Earrings

Don't have the patience to link together a whole bracelet or necklace? These earrings are the perfect way to try out the technique without investing too much time.

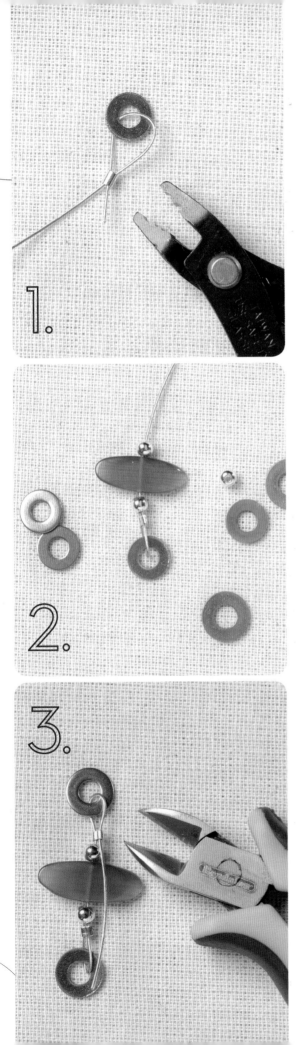

ONE: Crimp wire to washer

Begin making the first link by stringing an end of a wire section through a crimp tube and washer, then back through the crimp tube. Adjust the wire so the loop is approximately 1/4" (6mm) in diameter, then squeeze the crimp flat. Trim the short wire end with wire cutters. (See Techniques, page 139, for instructions on using a crimp tube.)

TWO: String beads onto wire

String the following sequence of beads onto the wire: silver bead, slide-cut glass cat eye bead, silver bead.

THREE: Finish link

To finish the link, string the wire through a crimp tube, then through a second washer. Thread the end back through the crimp, and adjust the wire to make another 1/4" (6mm) loop. Be sure there is no slack between the beads and the crimp before squeezing it closed. Trim the wire. Attach the next wire to this last washer and repeat steps 1 through 3 to create a new link. Repeat once more to create a total of 3 beaded sections connected by 4 washers.

TIP

Keep the size of your links consistent by comparing them to your first link before crimping them in place.

FOUR: Attach O-ring clasp component

Before attaching the O-ring section of the clasp, connect a fourth section of wire to the last washer and then string it with the bead sequence. Next string the wire through a crimp, then the O-ring clasp and back down through the crimp. Squeeze the crimp flat and trim the wire.

FIVE: Attach toggle clasp component

To attach the toggle section of the clasp, attach a fifth section of wire to the first washer, then string it with the following sequence of beads: silver bead, 4mm cat's eye bead, silver bead. Next string the wire through a crimp, then through the toggle and back down through the crimp. Squeeze the crimp flat and trim the wire.

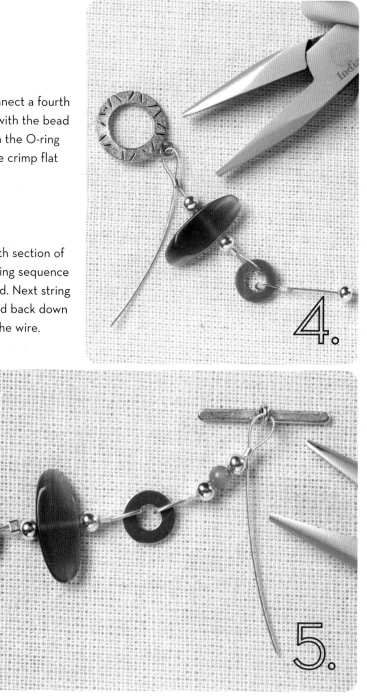

Quartz Hardware Set

This simple linking technique transfers easily to different-sized washers and beads. The trick is to balance the weight of your selections and keep the spacing consistent.

The pink quartz set features larger-sized washers to balance the rectangular beads. It takes eight sections of wire to make the links, plus an additional two to add a stylish question-mark-styled hook-and-eye clasp. I'd been hoarding these rose quartz beads in my beading stash since designing projects for *Simply Beautiful Beaded Jewelry,* but I had no idea how I was going to use them. I pulled them out and placed them against the washers, and I immediately loved the contrast of the rectangular shape with the round washers. I take this as proof that there's a reason to stock up on beads when you see them—you never know what project they'll complete.

EARRING TREE

Materials

* 4" (10cm) wooden square base
* 4¹/2" (11cm) long ¹/4" (6mm) diameter wooden dowel rod
* black-green and metallic silver acrylic paint (Delta Ceramcoat)
* foam brush
* 22- and 14-gauge galvanized steel wire (sold at hardware stores)
* old wooden spoon
* metal leaf charms and clasps (Blue Moon Beads)
* glass flowers
* wood glue

Tools: paintbrush, heavy-duty round-nose pliers, flat-nose pliers, wire cutters (mini-tool versions will not work on the heavy-gauge wire), drill and ¹/4" (6mm) bit

TIP

Do you have a big earring collection? Add a branch to your tree by increasing the height of the center dowel rod and adding an extra wire coil. However, you should be careful not to let your tree get too top heavy. It might be safer to create a small forest of trees than to overly distort the original dimensions.

If you're like me, you waste time every morning fishing around on your dresser top looking for a set of matching earrings. This easy-to-make earring tree will put an end to this search-and-match ritual by eliminating clutter and transforming your loose earrings into a beautiful focal point. You don't even have to thread earrings through holes. Drape them on the wire branches when you take them off and quickly snatch them off the branch when you're running out the door.

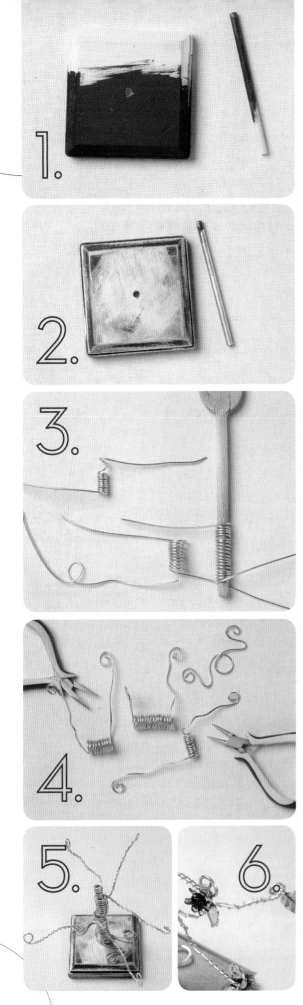

ONE: Drill and paint base and rod

Drill a hole halfway through the center of the wood base. The diameter of the hole should match the thickness of your dowel rod so that it slides into the hole and is relatively secure. The dowel rod will be glued in place at the very end. Paint the top and sides of the base and the dowel rod with black-green paint.

TWO: Dry brush on silver

With a dry brush, apply a light coat of silver paint over the black-green base coat. Leave some of the base coat exposed.

THREE: Twist wire for tree

The tree consists of 4 14-gauge wire pieces. For the first piece, make a single center loop in a 10" (25cm) wire section for the tree roots. To make the second piece, for the trunk, leave 2½" (6cm) of wire for a "root" and then wrap the wire 19 times around the handle of an old wooden spoon. Leave 5" (13cm) of uncoiled wire at the end for the first branch, then cut the wire. Slide the coil off the spoon handle and compress it into a tight spring by pushing the top and bottom ends together. Make a second pair of branches, leaving 4½" (11cm) at the end for another branch. Coil the wire 11 times, and leave an additional 4¼" (11cm) at the end for another branch. Trim the wire and compress the center coils. To make the top pair of branches, coil the wire around the leftover dowel rod. Leave a 4" (10cm) branch end, coil it 9 times, and leave another 3½" (9cm) of uncoiled wire for another branch. Trim the wire and compress the coil.

FOUR: Coil ends of branches

Use round-nose and flat-nose pliers to spiral all the wire ends. The 3 root ends should form larger spirals than the branch ends. Pinch the branch wires every 1" (3cm) or so to make a better surface for the earrings to grab onto.

FIVE: Assemble tree

To assemble the tree, slide the post into the base. Slide the roots onto the rod, then the trunk, the large branch coil and the smaller branch coil. Use pliers to bend the top small branch coil over the top of the post to hold the tree coils in place. Once you've made any adjustments, lift the post out while holding the coils in place. Drop some wood glue into the hole and reinsert the post. Let it dry. Wrap 22-gauge wire around each of the branches, starting at the coil and finishing at the spiral. Trim all the wire ends.

SIX: Attach charms

Link metal leaf charms and glass flowers to each branch end.

WINDOW SCREEN BASKET

Materials

* 12" x 24" (30cm x 61cm) piece of aluminum insect screen
* game piece beads, dice and dominos (Blue Moon Beads)
* 22-gauge plastic-coated Fun wire in pink, green, red and black (Toner Plastics)
* 2 binder clips or clothespins

Tools: scissors, wire cutters, round-nose pliers

Finished dimensions: 4¹/₂" high x 3¹/₂" x 4" (11cm x 9cm x 10cm)

Catch compliments—not bugs—with these unique vessels made with repurposed window screens. Stitch the folded screen with sections of plastic-coated wire. Use more wire to attach pre-drilled game pieces around the top edge of the wire basket to create a decorative border that also adds stability to the lightweight container.

Cylindrical Basket

Use a doubled rectangular piece of screen to make this cylindrical version. Roll the screen into a tube and fold the bottom edge into five equal wedges to make the base. Take small wire stitches to secure the shape, then finish the top edge of the basket using the same technique as used in the square basket.

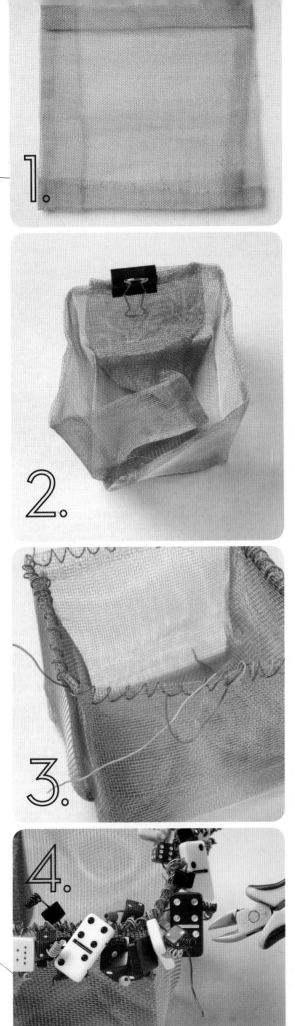

ONE: Prepare metal square

Fold the wire screen in half to make a 12" (30cm) square. Fold in 1" (3cm) of each cut edge. Press the folded edges flat with your hands.

TWO: Fold screen into square shape

Fold the screen in thirds, like folding a letter. Press the folds down to create crease lines, then unfold them. Rotate the screen and fold it in thirds again, pressing the folds down to create crease lines and then unfolding them. The fold lines create a rectangle in the center of the screen that becomes the base of the basket.

The 2 larger sides simply fold up and stay in place. The smaller sides fold up and overlap. You'll have extra screen material at the base of the smaller sides. Press the excess material into the basket to create a triangle on each side. Press the triangles flat against the base of the basket. Secure both sides of the basket with binder clips or clothespins.

THREE: Stitch around top of basket

Using a 14" (36cm) length of wire, begin stitching an overhand seam around the top ¼" (6mm) of the basket. The seam connects the overlapped screen and strengthens the top of the basket. Add more wire as you work to complete the seam. For extra stability, add a second seam in a contrasting color.

FOUR: Decorate top edge of basket

Cut the colored wires into 5" to 6" (13cm to 15cm) long segments. Thread a wire length halfway through the top of the basket, wrap 1 of the ends around the top of the basket to make a single overhand stitch. Thread a bead onto each wire end, tightly wrap the remaining wire around the round-nose pliers, slide out the pliers and press the coil against the bead. Repeat the process to distribute the different colored wires and game piece beads evenly around the top of the basket.

TIP

If you can't locate pre-drilled playing pieces, consider making your own by drilling holes in checkers and poker chips. Or wrap wire around chess pieces to hold them in place. Another option to consider is attaching a collection of plastic trinkets and toys, many of which have built-in openings that will accommodate the wire.

PLASTIC AND POLYMER

In this chapter, you'll feel like you're playing scientist as you learn to transform raw materials into unique hardened, wearable jewelry. No special tools or kilns are required—all you need is an electric drill and a stove.

I haven't met anyone who isn't entertained by witnessing a shrink sheet twist and curl to reduce size by twenty to forty percent. Shrink sheets are the perfect material for jewelry making—you have the luxury of decorating the material at its original size, but you can enjoy wearing it once it shrinks (see the *Shrink Art Earrings*, page 54). Casting resin jewelry is a simple chemistry process—the two-part solution cures to a clear solid resin that frames submerged messages and embellishments (see the *Cast Resin Charm Bracelet*, page 60).

Heat and resin make you nervous? The easiest way to incorporate plastic into your jewelry design is to simply drill a hole in a readymade material, and *voilá*, instant bead! Take the rubber *Safari Charm Bracelet*, for example (see page 52). Each miniature animal is drilled and strung onto a head pin. Each dangle is linked to a section of chain to make a one-of-a-kind charm bracelet.

Even credit cards are cut up, drilled and linked onto a chain bracelet (see page 64). In the case of the Playmobil jewelry (see page 50), the plastic flowers come ready to string. It makes you wonder what other jewelry-making treasures might be hiding in the bottom of the toy box.

If you haven't played with polymer clay, you're in for a real treat—it's like Play-Doh for grown-ups. Begin by kneading and conditioning the clay in your hands, then mold, cut, roll and shape it. A simple trip into the stove transforms your finished creation into hardened polymer. I've included three very different projects to get you started. The *Polymer Posies Barrette* (see page 66) teaches you to make a simple flower shape imbedded with wire and beads. The anime-inspired animal card pins (see page 74) are simply small clay shapes assembled to make miniature critters. The bookplate project (see page 70) is truly a mixed-media application. The clay is stamped, tinted with paint and embedded with a rhinestone. I hope one of these projects will get you hooked on this amazing product.

PLAYMOBIL EARRINGS

Materials

* 4 pink Playmobil flowers (or substitute plastic, glass or vintage Lucite flowers)
* 4 small freshwater pearls (Blue Moon Beads)
* 2 5" (13cm) lengths of pink 7-strand stringing wire (Beadalon)
* 2 crimp beads
* 2 clear pink E beads
* Beadfix glue (Beadalon)
* earring findings (Blue Moon Beads)

Tools: crimping pliers, wire cutters

Finished dangle length: 1¹/2" (4cm)

Making these earrings really is as easy as child's play. I love the idea of transforming children's toys into grown-up jewelry. The Playmobil company lends itself to this adaptation. They make beautiful, tactile toys in gorgeous colors with tons of little pieces. My version of finders-keepers is that if I've stepped on one of my kids' toys multiple times, I keep it. After all, will they really miss a few tiny flowers?

～ Playmobil Necklace

To make the necklace, pass two wire sections through a flower bead in opposite directions. Thread a bead onto each wire end, taping them in place as you work. Link as many flowers together as you like. Secure each bead with a drop of glue and add a clasp to finish the necklace.

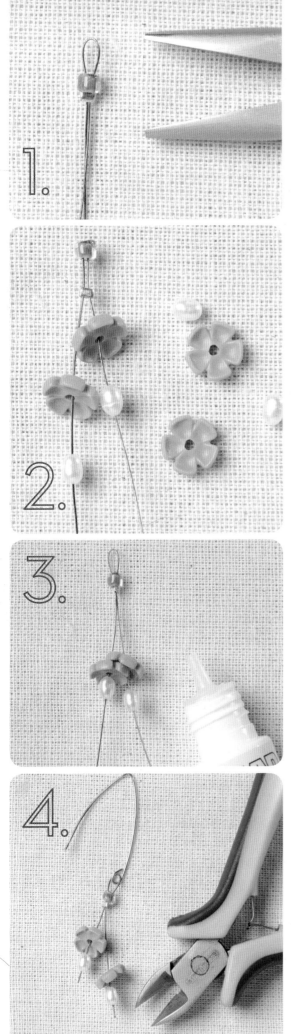

ONE: Secure bead
Fold 1 5" (13cm) length of stringing wire in half, and thread both ends through an E bead and a crimp bead. Slide the bead up ¼" (6mm) below the fold, then flatten the crimp to secure the bead in place.

TWO: Thread beads onto wires
Thread a flower followed by a pearl onto each wire end.

THREE: Apply glue to bottom bead
Squeeze a small amount of glue into either side of the opening in the pearl bead. Repeat for the second earring. Let the glue dry completely for 12 to 24 hours before handling the earrings.

FOUR: Finish earrings
Trim the wire ends ¼" (6mm) below the pearl beads. Hook the earring finding through the top loop of each finished flower dangle, using pliers to fully close the finding wire so that the cascade is trapped in place. Repeat for the second earring.

SAFARI CHARM BRACELET

Materials

* assortment of small rubber animals (sold in toy stores, Marco Polo)
* shell beads in oval amber, turquoise shell-and-resin chips, small oval ivory (Blue Moon Beads)
* flat round dark brown wooden beads (Blue Moon Beads)
* flat grey, 6mm round Bayong beads (Blue Moon Beads)
* matte metallic mix seed beads
* 7" (18cm) section of antique silver chain (Blue Moon Beads)
* antique silver head pins (Blue Moon Beads)
* antique silver jump rings
* antique silver lobster clasp

Tools: round-nose pliers, chain-nose pliers, wire cutters, drill and $^1/_{16}$" (1.5mm) bit, wood block

Finished length: 7$^1/_2$" (19cm)

Take a walk on the wild side with this playful bracelet. Drill miniature rubber animals and impale them on antique-finished head pins to make vibrant charms complemented by shiny natural shell and matte wood beads. If safari isn't your thing, you'll be pleased to know that little rubber pigs, lambs, chickens and even fiery dragons are widely available.

Frog Earrings

I can't wait to wear these frog earrings with my rubber boots in the late spring when we start to hear spring peepers as the sun sets. You can pierce tiny rubber animals with a straight pin instead of drilling them, although you may need pliers to help maneuver the pin.

ONE: Begin to make bead dangles

To make the first bead-dangle sequence, string three head pins with beads: 1 with a seed bead and the oval amber shell bead, the next with a seed bead and a square flat grey wood bead, the last 1 with a seed bead and a shell-and-resin chip.

TWO: Link dangles to chain

Create a wrapped loop above each bead. (See Techniques, page 140, for instructions on making a wrapped loop.) Hook all 3 dangles onto a jump ring and attach the ring to the fifth link on the chain. (See Techniques, page 141, for instructions on opening and closing a jump ring.)

THREE: Create second dangle sequence

To make the second, 2-dangle sequence, string 1 head pin with a seed bead and a round flat dark brown wood bead, and string the second with a seed bead, a round Bayong bead, an animal and a small ivory shell bead.

FOUR: Link dangles to bracelet

Make each of the head pins into dangles. Slide both dangles onto a jump ring. Leave an empty link after the first dangle, and then attach the 2 dangles to the next link. Skipping 1 link before placing a dangle ensures that all the dangles will hang down in the same direction. Repeat steps 1–4 until you've completed 5 animal-and-bead-dangle sequences. End with 1 more bead dangle sequence.

FIVE: Link clasp to bracelet

Slide the lobster clasp onto a jump ring and link it to the end of the chain. Hook the clasp to 1 of the 5 free links at the beginning of the bracelet.

· · · · · · · · · · · · **TIP** · · · · · · · · · ·

To drill the animals, work over a piece of scrap wood and drill a hole down the center of the animal. If the animal has a large head, like the lion, place the hole as close to the neck as possible to balance the weight. The alligator's weight is distributed evenly so you can place the hole in the real center of his body.

SHRINK ART EARRINGS

Materials

- inkjet shrink film (Grafix)
- 2 round green Swarovski crystal rounds
- 4 small lightweight bead caps (Blue Moon Beads)
- earring wires (Blue Moon Beads)
- 2 jump rings
- 2 eye pins
- clear acrylic stamps (Fiskars)
- permanent ink pad (StazOn)
- silver paint marker

Tools: scissors, ruler and pencil, computer and printer, standard hole punch, chain-nose pliers, round-nose pliers, wire cutters

Finished dangle length: 1/2" x 1" (1cm x 3cm)
Finished beaded length: 1 5/8" (4cm)

If you've never played with shrink art sheets, you're in for a crafting treat. Even if you're an experienced crafter, chances are you might not have tried this updated version. The sheet of shrink plastic runs right through your inkjet printer, enabling a wide variety of jewelry-making possibilities. I printed the pieces for these projects in a single color, then stamped them with permanent ink, punched holes in them and magically shrunk them in our countertop toaster oven.

Red Earrings

The red earrings are constructed the same way as the green pair. The image was originally a black and white photo of flowers that we altered to a very light red. The color significantly intensified during the shrinking process. To get this look, use slightly larger shrink sheet rectangles and don't round the corners.

ONE: Print images on shrink film and cut out

Begin by selecting an image to print onto the shrink film. Import the image into a program like Photoshop, then change the color by adjusting the hue saturation. The color will intensify when shrunk, so lighter coloration works best. The image on this earring is a line drawing of flowers that was altered to light green. Follow the package directions to print the image directly onto the shrink film. Use a pencil and ruler to measure out a 1¼" x 2½" (3cm x 6cm) rectangle for the earring dangle. The plastic shrinks to between 20 and 40 percent of its original size.

TWO: Round corners of rectangles

Use scissors to round the edges of the plastic pieces to give them a more finished look after they're shrunk.

THREE: Stamp rectangles

Working over a scrap piece of paper, stamp a message and designs onto the printed plastic.

FOUR: Punch holes

Use a standard hole punch to make a hole in each rectangle approximately ¼" (6mm) in from the edge. Shrink the plastic according to the package directions.

FIVE: Color back and edges of baked pieces

Apply silver paint marker to the edge and back of the shrunken pieces.

SIX: Link jump ring to dangle

Attach a jump ring through the hole in the top of each earring dangle. (See Techniques, page 141, for instructions on opening and closing a jump ring.)

SEVEN: Link earring components

String the following sequence of beads onto an eye pin: bead cap, crystal bead, bead cap. Make a wrapped loop above the beads. (See Techniques, page 140, for instructions on making a wrapped loop.) Link the bottom of the eye pin to the jump ring and the top of the eye pin to the earring finding.

TIP

I have the most success shrinking the piece in a preheated conventional oven. Some people use an embossing tool instead, but it can be difficult to get even heat distribution. Instead of shrinking uniformly, the piece tends to distort.

More Shrink Art Jewelry

Before printing your next sheet of plastic, alter the color of the image to completely change the appearance of your shrink art jewelry. For an extra colorful bracelet or necklace, choose a color of suede lace to match. You can also poke additional holes into the plastic prior to shrinking so you can add charms and beads to the finished piece.

Purple Prose Necklace

Be lovely in lavender in this necklace that bestows wishes of happiness, laughter and love on the wearer. Simply link spacers with jump rings and connect dangles to the center of each spacer. Add a beaded dangle and finish the suede ends with fold-over crimps linked to a simple clasp.

Charming Identity Bracelet

Individual crystal bead birthstones hang from this family-themed bracelet, making it the perfect Mother's Day gift. Loop a suede lace through either hole in this charm and finish the ends with fold-over crimps. Attach beaded dangles and a clasp to finish the bracelet.

MICRO BEAD CHARM NECKLACE

Materials

- silver metal photo frame (Blue Moon Beads)
- silver micro Liquid Beadz (DecoArt)
- sand dollar scrapbook embellishment
- 10 freshwater pearls (Blue Moon Beads)
- matte gold seed beads
- 18" (46cm) length of .018" (5mm) crinkle wire (Beadalon)
- 18" (46cm) length of gold .015" (4mm) stringing wire (Beadalon)
- silver clasp (Blue Moon Beads)
- jump rimg
- 2 crimp tubes

Tools: wax paper, plastic knife, wire cutters, crimping pliers

Finished length: 16³/4" (43cm)

I tried umpteen different ways of setting miniature photographs inside these frames, but the results just didn't thrill me. But when I smeared Liquid Beadz into the frame, I knew I was onto something. I couldn't believe my luck—the surface of the Liquid Beadz held the sand dollar charm in place. The juxtaposition of the three different metal colors and finishes works together to make a great pendant. Don't skip the Beadalon crinkle wire— it cleverly holds the freshwater pearls in place.

Bee Pendant

Gold Liquid Beadz is the perfect background for this charm. Use the same technique as for the sand dollar pendant, but use different colored micro beads and a different charm.

ONE: Spread liquid beads into frame

Working over a protected work surface such as wax paper, spread the liquid beads into the photo frame with a plastic knife.

TWO: Place sand dollar into wet beads

Place the sand dollar embellishment on top of the wet beads and press down firmly so the beads nestle around its edges to anchor it in place. Allow the charm to dry overnight.

THREE: String necklace

String 8" (20cm) of seed beads onto the gold stringing wire, and 5 pearls onto the crinkle wire. The pearls are a snug fit on the crinkle wire. Space them evenly over 8" (20cm). Hook a jump ring onto the finished charm and thread both wires through the ring. (See Techniques, page 141, for instructions on opening and closing a jump ring.)

FOUR: Attach clasp

Finish stringing the seed beads so you have a finished beaded length of 16" (41cm). Add 5 more pearls to the crinkle wire, again evenly spaced over 8" (20cm). Attach each clasp component to 1 end of the necklace with a crimp tube. (See Techniques, page 139, for instructions on using crimp tubes.) Trim the wires.

Heart Earrings

Fill heart charms with purple micro beads to make these simple earrings. Add any beads you like to finish the look.

CAST RESIN CHARM BRACELET

Materials

* ⁵⁄₈" (2cm) button covers (sold in the notions department of fabric stores)
* colored paper
* Valentine stickers (DK)
* rub-on or vellum words
* micro beads
* clear Swarovski crystal rhinestones
* Glossy Accents (Ranger Industries)
* pour-on high-gloss finish cast resin solution (Envirotex)
* 2 2¹⁄₂" (6cm) sections ¹⁄₈" (3mm) black rubber tubing
* 9" (23cm) length of stringing wire (Beadalon)
* heart toggle clasp (Blue Moon Beads)
* 4mm closed bumper ring (Beadalon)
* 2 jump rings
* pink glass beads
* 6mm glass pearl bead
* pink Swarovski crystal cube
* heart charm (tag from clasp set) (Blue Moon Beads)
* crimp tubes and crimp beads

Tools: tweezers, craft stick, drill and ¹⁄₈" (3mm) bit, chain-nose pliers, wire cutters

Finished length: 7" (18cm)

This charm bracelet turned out to be one of my favorite projects in the book. At first, I was a little apprehensive about using resin, but once I got the hang of it, thanks in large part to Sherri Haab's book, *The Art of Resin Jewelry*, I was hooked. Traditionally, bottle caps are used for the charm base, but I discovered that inverted button covers are smaller, smoother and have an attractive bezeled edge. The other bonus is they come in a package of six, and you don't have to empty the soda bottles before getting started!

~ Earrings

These earrings feature the same button covers in a smaller size. Make a statement by using two messages that read separately and as a pair.

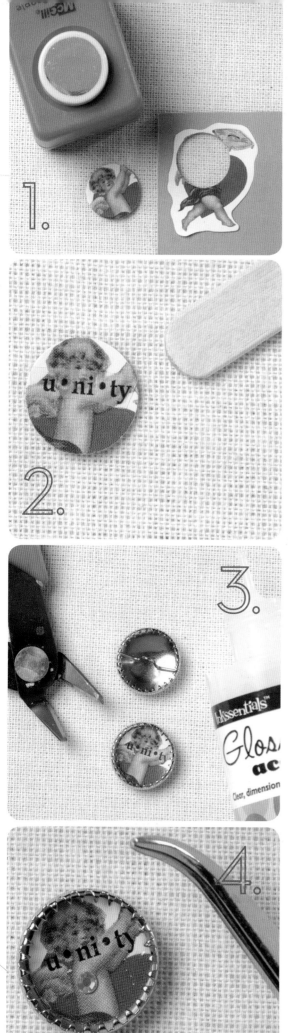

ONE: Punch out image

Punch a circle out of the colored paper or trace the button cover onto the colored paper and cut out the circle. Test fit the paper into the button cover, and remove and trim off any extra paper. Silhouette-cut the image out of the sticker, and then crop it to fit the circle. If you know the paper will fit perfectly, you can apply the sticker to the colored paper and punch out both together.

TWO: Apply letters or phrase to image

Use a craft stick to apply rub-on letters over the sticker image or use glossy glue to glue on cut vellum words.

THREE: Adhere image to button cover

Remove the center wire from the button cover with wire cutters. Use Glossy Accents to glue the paper circle into the button cover.

FOUR: Add rhinestone

Apply a protective coat of Glossy Accents over the image, and use tweezers to add a rhinestone. Let the glue dry.

FIVE: Mix resin and pour into button cover

When mixing resin, be sure to work in a warm, well-ventilated area over a surface protected with wax paper. Pull on the gloves and mix up the solution according to the package directions. Immediately pour it into the button cover. The resin will look bubbly and cloudy when you first pour it but should clear when it settles and hardens.

SIX: Add micro beads

Use tweezers and a toothpick to help place micro beads in the resin before the surface hardens. Do not disturb or agitate the surface, as that will cause bubbles. Let the resin cure completely for 24 hours.

SEVEN: Drill hole through charm

Place the cured charm on a wood block and drill a hole in the top. Thread a jump ring through the hole and close the ring. (See Techniques, page 141, for instructions on opening and closing a jump ring.)

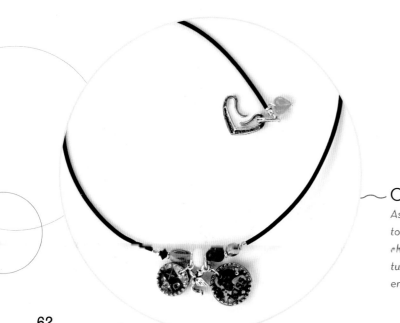

~ Cast Resin Necklace

Assemble the necklace like the bracelet. You'll need to add a second smaller cast resin charm and a cupid charm to enlarge the center motif. Substitute thinner tubing to make a graceful necklace, and fasten the ends with a heart toggle clasp.

EIGHT: Crimp clasp to wire end

Crimp 1 side of the clasp to an end of the stringing wire. (See Techniques, page 139, for instructions on using crimp tubes.) String on a bumper, a pearl and another bumper.

NINE: String on rubber tubing

String on a section of rubber tubing and another bumper.

TEN: String on bead and charms

String the crystal bead onto the wire. Link a second jump ring with a heart charm to the resin charm. String the charm onto the wire.

ELEVEN: Finish bracelet

String on another section of wire tubing and end with a bead. Crimp the clasp in place. Trim away the excess wire.

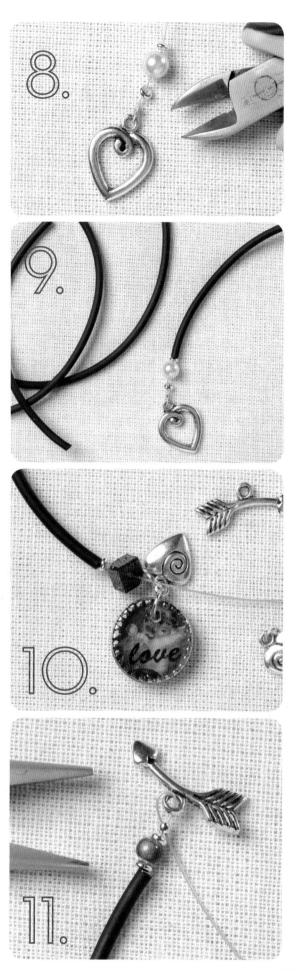

CREDIT CARD BRACELET

Materials

* 5 or 6 old expired credit cards or plastic gift cards
* assorted children's plastic beads
* 7¼" (18cm) large circle link chain (Blue Moon Beads), or 18 heavy-weight large jump ring links
* O-ring and toggle clasp

Tools: drill and ¹⁄₁₆" (2mm) drill bit, wood scrap, scissors, chain-nose pliers, round-nose pliers

Finished length: 8½" (22cm)

TIP

Gift cards work just as well as credit cards and come in equally unique colors and patterns. Once you've used up the credit, hold onto the card for crafting. If you're lucky, it should be easy to collect enough cards to make a bracelet around the holidays.

Cutting up charge cards to use them in this bracelet is probably the best choice I've made with credit cards. It protects old cards from identity theft, and if you wear it when you're out shopping, it's a not-so-subtle reminder to keep spending under control. With a sharp pair of scissors, simply cut up cards into fun rounded shapes then drill holes in them so they can be easily strung onto the open links of a wide chain. Plastic beads add dimension and whimsy while keeping the finished bracelet lightweight and comfortable to wear. If you've ever signed up for cards just because they look pretty, here's the perfect way to recycle them.

ONE: Cut up cards

Use sharp scissors to cut the credit cards into ½" to 1" (1cm to 3cm) rounded boomerang shapes. (This shape is like a triangle with a rounded V cut from the bottom.)

TWO: Drill holes

Working over a wood scrap, drill 1 hole in each plastic piece. Vary the location of the holes, with some on the ends and others in the center.

THREE: String plastic pieces onto links

Open a chain link laterally and remove it from the chain. (See Techniques, page 141, for instructions on opening and closing a jump ring.) String a dangle right side down followed by a second dangle right side up so the 2 pieces will swing with the wrong sides together.

FOUR: Add bead to link

String a bead onto the link and then use pliers to carefully close it, making sure the wire ends are locked together.

FIVE: Continue linking dangles to chain

Make another link following steps 3-4, but hook it onto the first link before closing it. Continue adding beaded dangle links until you have 18 linked rings that measure 7¼" (18cm).

SIX: Link clasp to chain

Attach 1 toggle clasp component to either end of the bracelet.

POLYMER POSIES BARRETTE

Materials

* fucshia (5504) and orange (5033) polymer clay (Premo, Sculpey)
* 2" (5cm) length of black 26-gauge wire
* turquoise bugle beads
* straight pin with round plastic end
* 1 barrette clip

Tools: wax paper or index card, round-nose pliers, wire cutters

Finished flower size: 3/4" (2cm)

Everything's coming up posies! You'll be surprised how quickly these cheerful little flowers will bloom over your work surface. This is the perfect beginner polymer clay project—the rolled petal shapes are easy to form and the size of the pieces simplifies the assembly. If you're already a polymer clay whiz, embedding the spiral wire centers and beaded details are great ways to experiment with adding elements to your clay work.

ONE: Begin to create flower

Condition the clay and roll it into a 1/8" (3mm) snake on wax paper or an index card. Starting at 1 end, begin folding the coil into 3 continuously connected 1/4" (6mm) petals.

TWO: Finish petals

Form 3 more equal-sized petals, and trim off any remaining clay. Connect the last petal to the first to make a flower shape.

THREE: Finish flower shape

Slide the round end of the straight pin down the center of each of the petals to blend the fold line and give the appearance of a solid petal with a center indentation.

FOUR: Add flower center

Roll orange clay into a ball about the size of a pea, place it in the center of the petals and press it flat.

FIVE: Add bugle beads

Carefully place a bugle bead in the center of each petal, positioning them as close to the orange flower center as possible.

SIX: Add wire spiral

Using round-nose pliers, shape the wire into a spiral. Fold the outside end down at a 90-degree angle. Trim the end so that it's ¼" (6mm) long, and then press the end down into the flower center.

SEVEN: Glue flower to barrette

Bake the flower according to the package directions. Once it's cooled, glue it to an opened clip. Be careful to position the flower towards the end so it doesn't interfere with the clip's spring action.

More Polymer Posies

Once you've got the knack for rolling up these little blossoms, it's hard to stop—especially with so many color choices at your fingertips. This three-strand polymer posy necklace and bright hair clips are great ways to showcase your handiwork.

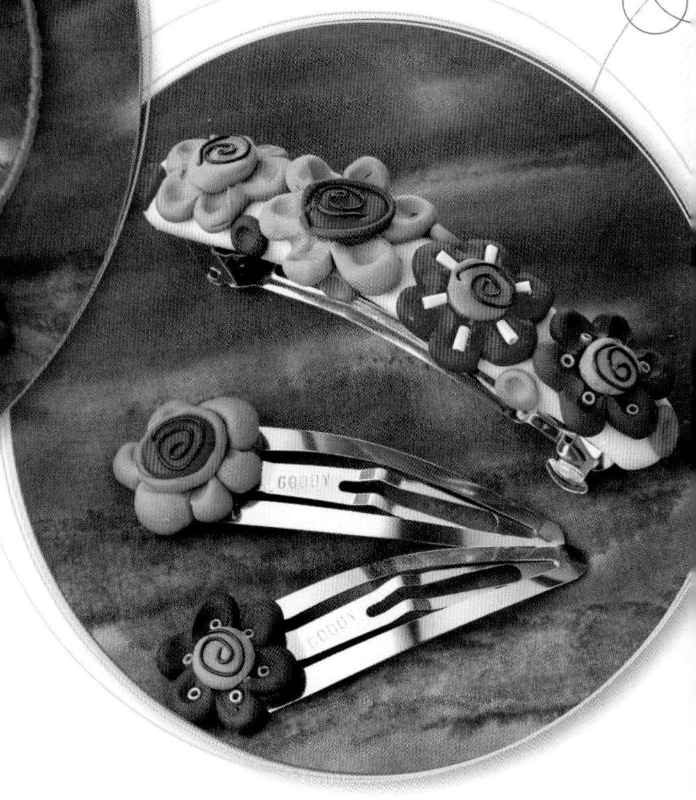

Polymer Posy Necklace

When it comes to posies, less is definitely not more. Don't stop with just one flower. A grouping of three different colored flowers strung with different colored beads makes a charming necklace. To create this necklace, make the flowers as for the barrette, except poke a trimmed head pin vertically down the center of each flower before baking. Each strand is strung with a different variety of seed or bugle beads. Select one strand to have a flower in the center. The other two strands will have a flower positioned slightly off center to the left or right. Be sure to stop stringing each strand at the right location to place a flower pendant. Use a large crimp tube to attach a single hook-and-eye clasp to all three strand ends.

Polymer Posy Barrettes and Hair Clip

These little posies are so versatile, you can find lots of ways to use them. In the hair clip shown here, I applied a layer of white polymer clay over the barrette back and then pressed four flowers onto the top of the clay. I filled in the design with rolled colored spots. The small barrettes are variations on the project shown on pages 66-68.

POLYMER CLAY BOOKPLATE NECKLACE

Materials

* brushed metal bookplates
* translucent polymer clay (Premo, Sculpey)
* crystal AB rhinestone
* black glass leaf beads
* copper colored glass flower bead
* 8mm red pearl
* garnet stone chips
* 2 5$\frac{1}{2}$" (14cm) sections and 1 3-link section of antique silver bike chain (Blue Moon Beads)
* .015" (4mm) stringing wire (Beadalon)
* antique silver lobster clasp (Blue Moon Beads)
* 3 head pins
* 2 antique silver jump rings
* 2 antique silver crimp beads (Blue Moon Bead)
* 2 4mm and 3 6mm antique silver jump rings (Blue Moon Beads)
* burgundy, copper and silver acrylic paint
* stamps (Fiskars Clear Romance)
* permanent black ink pad (StazOn)
* Glass Bead glue (Aleene's)

Tools: clay roller, wax paper or index card, paper towel, craft knife, paintbrush, twist ties, crimping pliers, chain-nose, round-nose pliers, wire cutters

Finished length: 17" (43cm)

Scrapbooking bookplates make the perfect frames for polymer clay. They frame the embellished clay while also protecting it and strengthening the vulnerable edges. The predrilled holes make it easy to embellish the finished piece with beads, chain and wire. In this necklace, the translucent clay center has been stamped, embedded with rhinestones and tinted with acrylic paint. I love the way the light shines through the layers. I've just scratched the surface of this technique—different base clay colors, pigments and stamps will create different centerpieces to your jewelry.

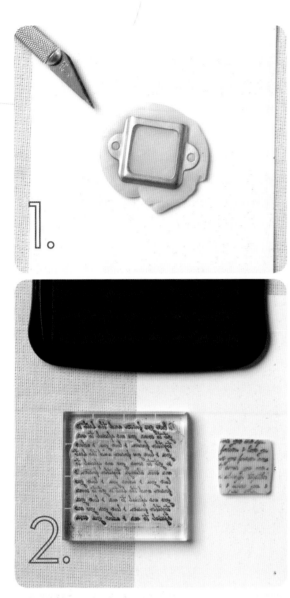

ONE: Cut clay to fit bookplate

Working over wax paper or an index card, condition and roll the clay to ¼" (6mm) thick. Press the bookplate into the clay to mark the exact size. Cut out the inside square with a craft knife.

TWO: Stamp clay

Ink the stamp with a black ink pad and press it lightly into the cut-out clay square.

THREE: Emboss heart in clay

Press the plain heart stamp into the clay over the stamped words to make an embossed image.

FOUR: Embed rhinestone in clay square

Place a rhinestone in the top center of the heart, and press it into the clay with the rounded tip of the pin. Sandwich the finished clay between 2 bookplates. Bake the clay inside the metal bookplates according to the package directions. Let it cool completely.

FIVE: Paint baked square

Remove the bookplates, and brush the stamped surface with burgundy paint. Immediately use a paper towel to rub off the wet paint, leaving a light stain. Brush copper paint into the embossed heart, and then gently rub off the paint that is resting above the embossed pattern. Dampen the paper towel to remove any paint you're unhappy with, and then reapply.

SIX: Secure bookplates with glue

Apply glue around the edge of the clay, and replace the metal bookplates. Use twist ties to join the top and bottom of the plates firmly together while the glue dries.

SEVEN: Add dangles to pendant

To finish the pendant, add a jump ring to the top and bottom loops in the bookplate. (See Techniques, page 141, for instructions on opening and closing a jump ring.) String each head pin with a bead and create a wrapped loop above each bead. (See Techniques, page 140, for instructions on making a wrapped loop.) Link 2 beaded head pins and the top link of the 3-link chain section to the jump ring at the bottom of the bookplate. Connect the last beaded head pin to the end of the small chain section.

EIGHT: Link chain section to stringing wire

Use a crimp bead to attach the stringing wire to the last link in the 5½" (14cm) chain section. (See Techniques, page 138, for instructions on using crimp tubes.)

NINE: Bead wire

String the wire with 3" (8cm) of garnet stone chips, then string on the finished pendant. String on 3" (8cm) more of stone chips.

TEN: Finish necklace

Crimp the wire to the second 5½" (14cm) chain section. Attach 4mm jump rings to the open chain ends, and hook a lobster clasp onto 1 of the rings.

POLYMER PIN ANIMAL CARDS

Materials

* white (5001) and black (5042) polymer clay (Premo, Sculpey)
* Ultralight polymer clay (Sculpey)
* tie tack pin
* purple cardstock
* patterned green scrapbook paper
* light brown scrapbook paper
* light green vellum
* origami paper
* Glass and Seed Bead glue (Aleene's)
* Glossy Accents (Ranger)

Tools: scissors, wax paper, toothpick, pencil

Finished animal size: ¾" (2cm)

These little critters are irresistible to both young and old alike. Each pin is outfitted with a tie tack so it can be easily transferred to clothing or accessories. Don't be discouraged by the miniature details—every little step has been broken down, making the animals easy to recreate. This project is a card and a gift all in one. While you have the supplies out, make a few extra and keep them on hand for a gift-giving emergency.

Bunny and Squirrel Pins

Once you get a feel for modeling the panda, it'll be easy to make the simple adapations to create a happy bunny or a spunky squirrel. Check out page 77 for the instructions on making these other animal variations.

1.

ONE: Make bear's head and body

With very clean hands, mix a generous pinch of Ultralight with regular white Premo. The Ultralight will lighten the finished pin so it doesn't pull on clothing. Manipulate the clay until it's well integrated and pliable. Roll an approximately 2¼" (6cm) ball for the body and a smaller, flatter pea-sized ball for the head. Press the head squarely into the body to fuse the clay pieces together.

2.

TWO: Make arms and legs

Wash your hands again to remove any traces of the white clay. Begin conditioning a pinch of black clay. To make a leg, roll out a ¼" (6mm) thick coil. Cut off a piece that's about 1" (3cm) long. Bend the center of the clay to make the knee, and round an end to form it into a foot. Gently pinch the other end to flatten it into a thigh. Repeat to make a second leg. The arms are made similarly to the legs, except the coil is ⅛" (3mm) thick and ¾" (2cm) long. Place a bend in the center for the elbow, form an end into a tapered hand, and flatten the other end for the shoulder connection. Repeat to make a second arm.

3.

THREE: Add arms and legs to body

Place the legs on either side of the body, positioning the left leg to drape over the front of the body and the right leg attached at the back of the body with the foot extending out from the side of its stomach. Attach the left arm over the front of the body, and attach the right arm over the other side. The hands shouldn't touch—leave some white belly exposed between them. Once you're pleased with the positioning, press the thigh and shoulder connections firmly into the white clay to better fuse them together.

4.

FOUR: Make ears, eyes and nose

You'll need to use tiny pieces of clay to make the ears, eyes and nose. Roll 2 balls for the ears. Roll a coil for the eyes and cut off 2 miniscule sections. Roll a flattened ball for the nose. Use a toothpick to position and press these tiny pieces into the panda's head. Bake the bear according to the package directions. Once the panda has cooled, glue the pin to the back. Let him dry before handling him.

Enlarge templates for branches and leaves by 147%.

FIVE: Begin to create card

Glue a 4" x 1½" (10cm x 4cm) rectangle of striped scrapbook paper and another rectangle of origami paper cut to the same size side by side on the front of the card. Stamp the message on a 1½" x 1" (4cm x 3cm) rectangle of green vellum, and then glue it to the bottom right hand corner of the glued papers.

SIX: Adhere branch and leaves to card front

Use the templates on this page to cut out a branch and some leaves. Cut the branch out of light brown paper, and use green patterned papers to cut out 8 leaves. Glue the bamboo branch vertically across the colored papers. Glue a scattering of leaves sprouting out of the branch.

SEVEN: Add pin

Poke the pin back through the card to finish.

 **TIP**

You might find that your first animal is on the large size—mine was! Your second will be smaller. Give yourself a chance to get used to the scale of the project.

More Polymer Pin Animal Cards

Don't stop with just one little critter! Follow these steps to make an irresistible bunny and squirrel to keep him company. Once you get a feel for how these animals are assembled, it should be relatively easy to translate your family's and friends' favorite animals into adorable wearable pieces. I'd love to try and miniaturize this design to make itty bitty earrings.

Bunny Card

Know someone who needs a little sunshine? Make this springtime bunny to help brighten her day. The flower is a simple circle cut from scrapbook paper.

Mix ecru clay with Ultralight clay to make the bunny's head and body. Orient the body upright. Mix raw sienna clay with the ecru to make the bunny's arms, legs, ears, eyes and nose. Add a little white tail that peaks out by his thigh.

Pair three paper strips together to make the background. Stamp the message directly onto the card. Cut a 1½" (4cm) circle out of scrapbook paper. Cut the leaf and a ¼" (6mm) wide stem out of green vellum.

TIP

If you're planning to mail your pin card, take precautions to protect the pin. Place corrugated cardboard inside the card so the pin back doesn't puncture it. Wrap the pin with bubble wrap and use a sturdy shipping envelope to send it off.

Squirrel Card

When fall is in the air, make this little squirrel for students and teachers heading back to school. You can make the tree and leaves from almost any paper scraps you might have on hand.

Use silver clay in addition to the colors from the other animals. Mix Ultralight clay into the silver clay to make the body, head and tail pieces. The arms, legs and ears are made with plain silver clay. The arms are only ⅜" (1cm) long and the legs are ⅝" (2cm) long with a single bend at the foot and hand. The tiny acorn is made with beige and brown clay left over from the bunny. Use a straight pin to crosshatch the acorn cap. Pair three horizontal paper strips together to make the background. Stamp the message on another horizontal vellum strip. Cut the trunk out of brown scrapbook paper and the leaves out of green vellum.

PAPER AND
CHARMS

I love the simple logic of the childhood rock, paper, scissors game—especially how the lightweight paper beats rock by covering it up. In this chapter, you'll see the amazing jewelry-making possibilities of paper. A simple application of Glossy Accents or Triple Thick hardens any paper creation so that it can be worn and enjoyed. Get started by simply rolling paper strips around a toothpick to make paper beads (see the *Rolled Paper Loop Earrings*, page 82). Or pull out your scrapbook paper stash and cut out simple pattern pieces to assemble a unique flower pin (see page 86). The *Paper Charm Earrings* (see page 80) are my personal favorites. Tiny decorative paper scraps are glued together, outfitted with eyelets and combined with beads to make lightweight earrings.

Although charms don't figure into the traditional rock-paper-scissors equation, in my book they're winners any day. Sometimes a charm throws me off my rocker and becomes the inspiration for an entire design. I loved the handcrafted look of a simple metal heart charm and chose to make it a pendant (see page 92) in one of the designs in this chapter. I paired it with sturdy stone beads, freshwater pearls and random metal beads to balance its weight. The starfish charm begged to be nestled in grains of sand, so I strung it on multiple strands of seed and E beads in colors found along the shoreline (see page 98). The red coral and jade stone beads were a natural pairing with heavy coins in the *Chinese Charm Necklace* (see page 94). Both the stone and metal elements were large, so I used tiny red seed beads and shimmering green E beads for contrast. In the *Three-Strand Charm Necklace* (see page 90), I intentionally spotlighted the small bead charms by stringing them on long, thin strands of seed beads.

The trick to winning this design game is to consider your elements, complementing and contrasting them as needed. Sometimes the solution is obvious—other times you need to try the unexpected and break the rules. Playing with beads still feels like a childhood game to me, but the props are better!

PAPER CHARM EARRINGS

Materials

- 2 5/8" x 1 1/8" (6cm x 3cm) rectangles of purple dimensional paper
- 2 1/2" x 1" (6cm x 3cm) rectangles of dark purple paper
- 2 3/8" x 15/16" (6cm x 3cm) rectangles of blue printed paper
- printed words cut from scrapbook paper
- moon charms (Blue Moon Beads)
- 6mm purple glass bead
- yellow star glass bead
- yellow drop-shaped glass bead
- 1/8" (3mm) eyelets
- antique silver earring findings (Blue Moon Beads)
- 2 antique silver eye pins
- 2 6mm antique silver jump rings
- Aleene's craft glue
- Triple Thick Glaze

Tools: wax paper or index card, 1/8" (3mm) hole punch, instant setter, scissors, round-nose pliers, chain-nose pliers, wire cutters

Finished dangle length: 2" (5cm)

I'll give you the stars, the sky and the moon … if I can make them out of paper! Even the tiniest of paper scraps and messages can simply be glued together, and when the protective coating hardens, you're left with fantastic jewelry. To make these earrings, set eyelets into the base piece of layered paper, then embellish the layered paper with findings, charms and beaded dangles. Once you've tried this technique, I guarantee you'll never look at a paper scrap the same way.

Love Earrings

The Love Earrings feature cut-out heart scrapbook paper. They have a single punch in the top and are connected to the fishhook earring finding with an eye pin threaded with a 4mm opaque red glass bead.

ONE: Stack and glue papers

Glue the paper pieces together with the largest piece on the bottom and the smallest piece on top. Center each rectangle on top of the previous piece. Repeat for the second earring.

TWO: Punch holes in paper pieces

Adhere a small cut-out phrase to the center of each layered piece. Position a hole punch over the paper where you want to make the hole. Hit the punch with a small hammer to make the hole. Position the holes close to the edge, but not close enough that the hole will tear open the bottom edge.

THREE: Apply glaze to paper pieces

Working over a piece of wax paper or an index card, brush glaze onto the punched rectangle. Let the first side dry before flipping the piece over and applying glaze to the other side. Continue applying coats of glaze until you're happy with the feel of the charm. Repeat for the second earring.

FOUR: Set eyelets in paper pieces

Set an eyelet in each of the punched holes, pushing each eyelet through the right side. Set the charm right-side down on a protected surface and use the setter to flatten the backs of the eyelets.

FIVE: Connect earring components

To make the beaded dangle, slide a purple bead onto an eye pin and turn a loop above the bead. (See Techniques, page 140, for instructions on turning a loop.) Hang the moon charm from the bottom loop. Link the beaded dangle to the bottom eyelet hole with a jump ring. (See Techniques, page 141, for instructions on opening and closing a jump ring.) Thread the earring finding through the top hole. Repeat with star and teardrop beads to finish the second earring.

ROLLED PAPER LOOP EARRINGS

Materials

* ⅛" x 9½" (3mm x 24cm) strips of black-and-white scrapbook papers (DCWV, Provo)
* 4mm clear AB Swarovski crystal bicones
* 4mm pink Swarovski crystal rounds
* 6mm black AB Swarovski crystal spacer beads
* silver seed beads
* 2 5½" (14cm) lengths of silver-plated stringing wire (Beadalon)
* earring findings (Beadalon)
* 2 black crimp beads
* Aleene's craft glue
* Triple Thick Glaze (DecoArt)

Tools: paintbrush, toothpicks, round-nose pliers, chain-nose pliers, wire cutters

Finished dangle length: 1½" (4cm)

These dangle earrings have presence, but they don't weigh down your earlobes. These earrings feature a larger rolled paper bead bracketed by pink, black, clear and silver beads. String both the paper and crystal beads onto a small section of lightweight silver stringing wire. The wire ends come together with the help of a crimp bead to form a hanging loop.

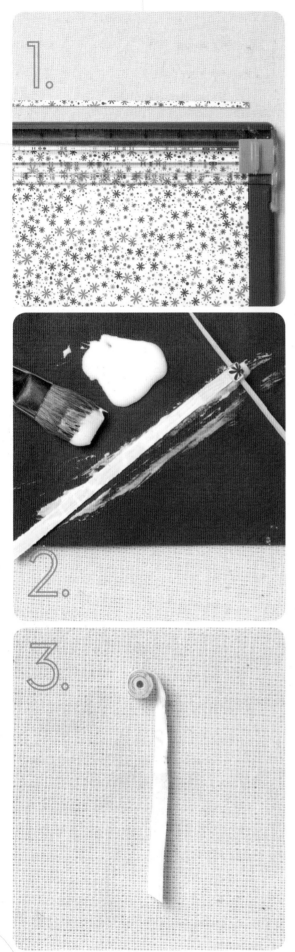

ONE: Cut paper strips

Use a paper trimmer to cut several 1/8" (3mm) strips of paper. Wider strips make a wider bead, and longer strips make a thicker bead.

TWO: Roll up paper strips

Working over wax paper or a piece of scrap paper, brush glue onto the back of a paper strip. Place the toothpick at 1 end and tightly roll the paper into a bead.

THREE: Finish rolling bead

Once the bead is started, you can pull out the toothpick and continue rolling. Add another drop of glue to the end of the paper strip so the bead doesn't unravel. Repeat steps 1 through 3 to make as many beads as you like. Set the beads aside to dry.

FOUR: Apply glaze to beads

Transfer the rolled paper onto a straight pin or a wire rack, and brush glaze onto all sides of the beads. Let them dry, and then reapply the glaze 1 to 2 more times. Set aside the beads to dry.

FIVE: String beads onto wire

String the following sequence of beads onto a section of lightweight stringing wire: silver seed bead, clear crystal bicone, pink round crystal, black crystal spacer, rolled paper bead, black crystal spacer, pink round crystal, clear crystal bicone, silver seed bead.

SIX: Secure loop with crimp bead

Fold the wire in half and bring both ends through a single black crimp bead. Bring 1 wire end back through the crimp bead, leaving a small loop above the crimp. Flatten the crimp bead with chain-nose pliers and cut away the excess wire with wire cutters. Attach the loop at the top of the dangle to an earwire. Repeat steps 1 and 2 to make the second earring.

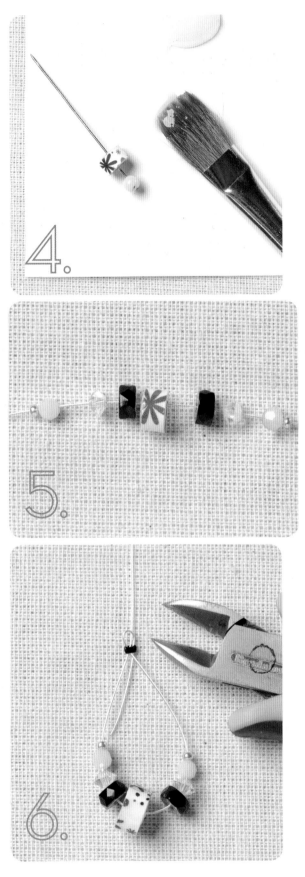

Rolled Paper Dangle Earrings

Materials

* 2 ½" (6cm) rolled paper beads (see page 82)
* 2 6mm pink faceted cat's eye beads (Beadalon)
* 2 4mm black Swarovski crystal bicones
* 2 pink seed beads
* earring findings (Beadalon)
* 2 head pins
* Aleene's craft glue
* Triple Thick Glaze (DecoArt)
* paintbrush
* toothpicks
* wax paper or scrap paper
* straight pin (optional) or wire bead baking tray (or use wire length)

Tools: crimping pliers, wire cutters

Finished dangle length: 1⁵/₈" (4cm)

If you've ever messed around with a paper strip, you've most likely begun making a rolled paper bead. The finishing step is to apply glue that hardens into a protective coating. You can recycle any paper scrap: The thickness, length and pattern of the strip determine the finished shape, size and color of the bead. I stuck with heavily patterned black-and-white scrapbook paper strips to give the finished bead an interesting surface design that works well with pink, turquoise and clear crystals.

ONE: String beads onto head pin

String the following sequence of beads onto a head pin: pink seed bead, black bicone crystal, rolled paper bead, faceted cat's eye bead.

TWO: Create dangle

Create a wrapped loop above the beads and trim away the excess wire. (See Techniques, page 140, for instructions on making a wrapped loop.) Hook the finished dangle to an earring finding. Repeat to make the second earring.

85

PAPER PETAL PIN

Materials

- 6" (15cm) square designer paper pad (Basic Grey)
- 3 2½" (6cm) sections of 22-gauge pink wire
- metallic gold seed beads
- felt scrapbook flower embellishments
- orange and crystal AB flat-backed round Swarovski crystals
- pin back
- Platinum Bond Glass and Bead Glue (Aleene's)
- craft glue (Aleene's)
- Triple Thick Glaze (DecoArt)

Tools: toothpick, paintbrush, wax paper or index card, round-nose pliers, scissors

Finished size: 2" (5cm) high x 2½" (6cm)

This ornate flower is a mixed-media creation that combines patterned paper, felt, wire, seed beads and rhinestones. Pattern pieces eliminate the guesswork—just cut the petal pieces out of scrapbook paper and stack them together. A triple-thick adhesive strengthens the paper so the finished pin is durable enough to wear on a coat or jacket.

⁓ Brown and Pink Pin

There's a second set of pattern pieces to create this flower (see page 142). The paper you select will dramatically change the appearance of your flower. Cut the pattern pieces out of different paper designs and experiment with color combinations by placing the shapes together. Once you find the arrangement that suits your style, apply the glue and embellishments.

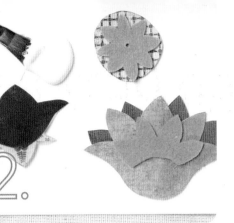

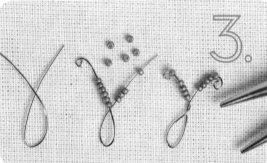

ONE: Cut out pieces and glaze

Using the template on page 142, cut the flower shapes out of colored paper. Working over wax paper or an index card, brush 2 coats of glaze onto each piece. Set the pieces aside to dry.

TWO: Adhere petal pieces together

Glue petal piece 2 over petal piece 1, then glue half of a large felt flower over the top half of piece 2. Glue petal 4 over leaf piece 5. Glue a small felt flower over flower center piece 3.

THREE: Make wire-and-bead stamens

Gently loop each section of pink wire in half to create a center loop. String 5 or 6 seed beads onto each wire end. Use round-nose pliers to turn the end of the wire into a loop that will pre-vent the beads from sliding off. Twist the wire once at the top of the loop to secure the beads. Repeat to make 3 beaded stamens.

FOUR: Adhere all flower pieces together

Glue the wire flower stamens over the felt-covered piece 2. Glue the combined pieces 4 and 5 over the bottom of the felt-covered flower center (piece 3).

FIVE: Add crystals

Use a toothpick to apply small dots of clear jewelry glue to the center of each petal in piece 2. Press an orange crystal into each glue dot. Apply more glue along the edge of petal 4, and press clear AB crystals into the glue.

SIX: Add pin back

Glue the pin back vertically down the back of the flower, and then glue a small felt flower over the connection to help strengthen the bond. Allow the pin to dry before wearing it.

TIP

You can easily modify this design to use it as a scrapbook page embellishment by removing some of the bulky felt layers.

CELL PHONE CHARM

Materials

- metal message beads (Blue Moon Beads)
- square polymer clay bead (Blue Moon Beads)
- 8mm turquoise round glass bead
- 4mm black AB Swarovski crystal round
- silver bead cap
- cell phone strap with attached ring (Beadalon)
- head pin

Tools: round-nose pliers, chain-nose pliers, wire cutters

Finished dangle length: 1½" (4cm)

Here's a quick and easy way to customize your phone. It's also the perfect project to showcase one-of-a-kind beads or message beads. No matter what you put your phone through, the looped cord ensures that your beading stays connected. Once you've made one cell phone charm, you'll start planning others for friends and family.

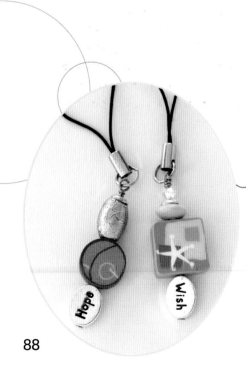

Gift Charm

Pair the perfect bead and message together to make a personalized gift charm. The pink hope charm was made in memory of a dear friend who passed of breast cancer last fall and lived every day with hope. For a more playful version, I paired the western star polymer clay bead with yellow and clear crystal beads and added the wish message bead for anyone with cowgirl dreams.

ONE: String beads onto head pin

String a metal message bead followed by the polymer clay bead onto a head pin.

TWO: String on more beads

Next add the turquoise bead, top it with a bead cap and end the dangle with a crystal bead.

THREE: Link dangle to cell phone strap

Create a wrapped loop above the beads and trim away the excess wire with wire cutters. (See Techniques, page 140, for instructions on making a wrapped loop.) Open the ring at the end of the cell phone strap laterally and hook the finished dangle onto the ring. (See Techniques, page 141, for instructions on opening and closing a jump ring.)

THREE-STRAND CHARM NECKLACE

Materials

- 26½", 33", 39" (67cm, 84cm, 99cm) strands of .015" (4mm) 49-strand stringing wire (Beadalon)
- solid and transparent turquoise, orange, red and silver seed beads
- foil turquoise E beads
- silver charm beads, including frogs, roses, birds, dragonflies and bunnies (Beadin' Path)
- assorted amber, red and turquoise glass beads
- 3-strand clasp
- crimp beads

Tools: crimping pliers, wire cutters

Finished length: 40" (102cm)

It's incredibly easy to incorporate these center-drilled metal charms into your beadwork. They string in place just like beads. I chose to frame each charm with two small silver seed beads and two foil-center E beads. The colorful background of small orange, blue and red seed beads complements the metal and highlights the assorted shapes of the charms.

Bunny Earrings

Center-drilled charms can easily be converted into dangles with the help of a head pin. Slide on the beads of your choice, and make a loop to link to an earring finding.

ONE: Begin to string beads

Tape 1 end of the shortest wire strand and start stringing approximately 2" (5cm) of a random assortment of seed beads (except for the silver). Then string on the following sequence of beads: silver seed bead, foil E bead, flower charm bead, foil E bead, silver seed bead. Use this sequence whenever you add a small charm.

TWO: Continue to string beads

String another 2" (5cm) of random seed beads, then string the following sequence of beads: silver seed bead, large glass bead, silver seed bead. When you string the larger charms, simply place them between the random strung seed beads. Continue stringing, alternating between the charm sequences and the glass bead sequence. Finish the strand with 2" (5cm) of seed beads and tape the end.

THREE: String longer strands

String the remaining 2 strands as you did for the first strand, always starting and ending the strand with 2" (5cm) of seed beads. Try to balance the beads and charms in varying locations along each strand.

FOUR: Attach clasp

Use crimp beads to attach 1 end of all 3 strands to 1 side of the clasp. (See Techniques, page 138, for instructions on securing wires with crimp beads.) Repeat to connect the other side of the strands with the other side of the clasp, making sure to pull the stringing wire tight before crimping.

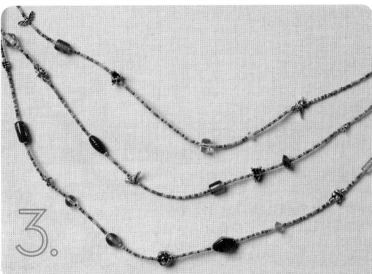

HAMMERED HEART NECKLACE

Materials

* heart charm (Blue Moon Beads)
* 4mm carnelian stone chip beads
* red glass flower and round beads
* 4mm topaz Swarovski crystal rounds
* 4mm olivine Swarovksi crystal bicones
* 4mm silver metal beads
* 4mm beige round glass beads
* silver E beads
* 6mm round jasper beads
* 8mm brown freshwater pearls (Blue Moon Beads)
* 8mm x 11mm green freshwater pearls (Blue Moon Beads)
* assorted silver metal dangles and beads (Blue Moon Beads)
* 18" (46cm) length of .015" (4mm) 49-strand stringing wire (Blue Moon Beads)
* silver metal clasp (Blue Moon Beads)
* 2 wire guardians
* 2 crimp beads

Tools: chain-nose pliers, wire cutters

Finished length: 17" (43cm)

I stumbled across this charm when I was opening a four-pack heart assortment. I was immediately drawn to its "handmade" chunky appearance. I decided to set it in an earthy mix of freshwater pearls, crystal, stone and glass beads. Peppered among the randomly strung beads are a few silver metal beads and dangles to help integrate the heart into the strand.

Flower Tag Earrings

The clasp from the heart necklace came with an unexpected bonus flower tag. Instead of using it with the clasp, I grabbed a second tag and made them the focal point for a pair of earrings. Of course, you can substitute any charm you have in your stash.

ONE: Attach clasp to wire

Thread the stringing wire through a crimp and wire guardian and then hook the strung guardian through the clasp. Thread the wire back down through the crimp. Remove any slack and flatten the crimp bead with chain-nose pliers. (See Techniquies, page 138, for instructions on using crimp beads.)

TWO: Begin stringing beads

Begin stringing a random mixture of all the stone, pearl, crystal and glass beads onto the wire. Separate the larger metal tag and bead elements by 1 1/2" to 2" (4cm to 5cm) of beading.

THREE: Finish stringing first half of necklace

Once you've beaded approximately 7 1/2" (19cm), you've reached the middle of the necklace. String on 4 E beads and the heart charm. Because of its large opening, the heart will swing freely over the E beads.

FOUR: Finish necklace

String the other half of the beads, and attach the other side of the flower clasp using another wire guardian and a crimp bead.

93

CHINESE CHARM NECKLACE

Materials

- small metal Chinese coin charms, with a small gold jump ring attached to each charm
- donut-shaped jade bead (Blue Moon Beads)
- flat coral disks (Blue Moon Beads)
- 10mm brown stone bead (Blue Moon Beads)
- 6mm dark red stone bead (Blue Moon Beads)
- irregular round jade bead (Blue Moon Beads)
- dark red seed beads
- gray and red foil E beads
- 20" (51cm) .018" (5mm) 49-strand gold-plated stringing wire (Beadalon)
- antique gold lobster clasp
- 6 gold crimp beads

Tools: chain-nose pliers, wire cutters

Finished length: 16¾" (43cm)

I created this set for my friend, Hannah, and her daughter, Nina, who has been with us for just over a year. I also drew inspiration from the wonderful line of Chinese charms from Blue Moon Beads that pair beautifully with natural coral and jade beads. Both the donut bead attachment technique and asymmetrical layout that breaks down into thirds can be easily adapted to other stone and bead varieties.

Chinese Charm Bracelet

The juxtaposition of large stone beads and small seed beads translates well in this bracelet variation. String the bracelet in three separate sections, then connect the strands with jade donut beads.

ONE: Begin stringing first section

1. Use a gold crimp bead to attach the clasp to the end of a 10" (25cm) strand of stringing wire. String 3" (8cm) of red seed beads onto the wire. String on a gray E bead followed by a red seed bead. Repeat the sequence 8 more times. (See Techniques, page 138, for instructions on using a crimp bead.)

TWO: Make loop with seed beads and jade donut

String the following beads onto the wire: 6mm round bead, flat coral disk, 10mm brown stone bead, 2 irregular jade beads, red foil E bead, crimp bead. Then string on approximately 20 red seed beads, followed by a donut-shaped jade bead. Bend the stringing wire back through the crimp bead. The seed beads should create a comfortable loop around the jade bead. If necessary, add or remove seed beads before flattening the crimp bead.

THREE: Begin beading next section

Cut 10" (25cm) of stringing wire. String a crimp bead onto 1 end of the wire, then pass the wire through the center of the jade donut. Pass the end back through the crimp bead and squeeze the bead flat with chain-nose pliers. Bead this second strand similarly to the first strand: 1½" (4cm) of red seed beads, 6mm red stone bead, jade bead, charm, 2 10mm brown stone beads, 3 coral beads, red foil E beads, 3 jade beads, *gray E bead, red seed bead. Repeat from the * 7 times. End this strand with 2" (5cm) more of seed beads, a crimp bead, and 20 more seed beads around a second jade donut. Secure the end by crimping it in place, as in step 2.

FOUR: Finish necklace

Crimp a third 4¼" (11cm) strand of stringing wire around the second donut, as in step 3. String the following sequence of beads onto the wire: red foil E bead, 2 jade beads, 6mm stone bead, gray E bead, 1½" (4cm) of red seed beads, crimp bead. String the wire through the other half of the clasp, and back down through the crimp. Squeeze the crimp closed to secure the strand.

BEADED COLLAGE WATCH

Materials

* square 3-strand watch face (Beadalon)
* assorted round, bicone and cube-shaped Swarovski crystal beads
* assorted red, blue, green, purple, amber and teal glass beads
* assorted silver, antique, silver and gold metal beads
* assorted silver dangles and bead caps
* 6 6" (15cm) lengths of .018" (5mm) 49-strand stringing wire (Beadalon)
* ornate 3-strand clasp (Blue Moon Beads)
* 6 wire guardians (Beadalon)
* 6 crimp tubes
* tape

Tools: chain-nose pliers, wire cutters, crimping pliers

Finished length: 7 1/4" (18cm)

I like to think of these pieces as collage beading—they're great for using leftover odds and ends. Choosing a limited color palette works best. I stuck with jewel tones of red, purple, turquoise and green with neutral complements. Even though the beads are randomly strung, the weight, texture and metal finishes are balanced among the strands. Wire guardians protect the wire where it's attached to the watch face.

Beaded Collage Earrings

Ornate flower head pins make these earrings a snap to assemble. Just string a few beads onto the head pin before looping the end. Hook the finished dangle onto an earring finding. If you're having difficulty finding decorative head pins, you can always string metal flower beads onto the end of a regular head pin.

ONE: String beads onto first strand

Determine how many inches (or centimeters) of beading you need between the watch face and the clasp—generally about 2¼" (6cm). Arrange a mixture of beads and thread them onto 1 strand. Tape the beads in place.

TWO: Bead all strands

Bead 2 more strands for 1 side of the watchband and another 3 strands for the other side.

THREE: Link beaded strands to watch face

Hook a wire guardian onto 1 of the outside rings of the watch face. Using a finished beaded strand, remove the tape and pass the stringing wire end through a crimp bead, through the wire guardian and back through the crimp bead. Repeat the process to attach the 5 remaining strands to the watch face. (See Techniques, page 138, for instructions on using a crimp bead.)

FOUR: Crimp strands in place

Use a crimp tube to attach each stringing wire end to the clasp, making sure to remove any slack before squeezing the tube shut with chain-nose pliers.

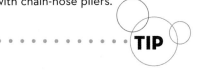

· · · · · · · · · · · · ·•**TIP**

The beads should appear random, but you'll need to offset the position of larger beads on one strand with smaller beads on the strands beside it. Also make sure the dangles and bead caps are evenly distributed throughout the strands for balance.

Beaded Collage Necklace

This necklace uses the same design concepts as the watch, but on a much smaller scale. Implement the same stringing strategies with the seed beads, distributing the colors evenly without using a predictable pattern. It might take a few tries to find the right combination of beads and dangles for the center section. Make sure you hold the necklace up and test how your design is hanging before beading the remaining half of the seed beads.

MULTISTRAND STARFISH NECKLACE

Materials

* starfish pendant (Blue Moon Beads)
* 3-hole silver ring (Blue Moon Beads)
* pearl seed beads
* pink, beige and aqua E beads
* 1 freshwater pearl
* 1 pink glass bead
* 4 $17^1/_2$" (44cm) strands of .015" (4mm) 49-strand bright stringing wire (Beadalon)
* $4^1/_2$" (11cm) length of imitation leather cord
* 3 links of silver metal chain (Blue Moon Beads)
* lobster clasp
* 2 fold-over crimps
* 2 lightweight head pins

Tools: round-nose pliers, chain-nose pliers, wire cutters

Finished length, including leather tie and clasp: 19" (48cm)

Like grains of sand on the beach, fine strands of seed and E beads are the perfect setting for this dramatic starfish charm. The strand ends are seamlessly joined together with the help of a fold-over crimp. The unexpected leather tie and bead dangle throw the design off center and add textural interest to the finished piece.

ONE: String first strand

Tape an end of 1 strand of stringing wire and string on 8¼" (21cm) of aqua E beads. Then thread the starfish charm onto the stand. String on another 8¼" (21cm) of aqua beads. Tape the end of the strand to secure the beads.

TWO: Continue stringing

Add 3 more strands of beads: 1 strand of beige E beads, 1 strand of pearl seed beads, and 1 strand of pink E beads. When you reach the middle of each strand, thread it through the starfish charm.

THREE: Secure strands in fold-over end

Working with 1 side at a time, bring all 4 strands together in a fold-over clasp. Use chain-nose pliers to fold down the metal sides, trapping the ends in place. Trim the ends with wire cutters. Repeat with the other side, making sure to remove any slack before closing the crimp.

FOUR: Link chain links to spacer

Hook 3 chain links to the center hole of the 3-hole ring, making sure to open and close the link laterally.

FIVE: Link clasp to chain

Add a lobster clasp to the open end of the chain. String the pearl onto a head pin, shape the end with round-nose pliers and hook it through a hole in the ring. Wrap the wire and trim away the excess with wire cutters. (See Techniques, page 140, for instructions on creating a wrapped loop.) Thread an aqua seed bead and a pink glass bead onto another head pin and create a dangle. Attach the dangle to the remaining hole.

SIX: Finish necklace

Slide the leather cording through the hole in the fold-over end and fold it in half. Bring both ends through the 3-hole ring and knot it in place. Fasten the lobster clasp by hooking it to the free fold-over end.

CRYSTAL AND
GLASS

Glass is quite amazing—it's hard to imagine what beading would be like without this wonderful material. If you've ever had the chance to make glass beads or watch someone else make them, you know how fascinating it is to see glass being molded into a finished object.

I love to discover new glass beads that inspire projects, which is exactly what happened when I came upon opaque glass flower and leaf beads at our local bead store, the Beadin' Path. I was taken in by their vintage appearance, and to showcase them I designed a *Flower Vine Choker* (see page 108) where each shaped bead is suspended from the end of a miniature stem. Another design inspiration came from placing unlikely colors and shapes of glass beads together. The *Teardrop Necklace* (see page 110) is all about contrast. Two vibrant strands of clashing colors work surprisingly well together in organic and square shapes. The finished design is punctuated with sparkling round crystals.

Genuine crystal beads are actually machine-cut lead glass. Each of the tiny cuts refracts the light. The *Crystal Ball Earrings* (see page 102) are the epitome of crystal sparkle. Bicone crystal beads are cleverly wired together to make an eye-catching sparkling ball, which can be hung on an earring finding or take center stage as a pendant. I also have to mention my dazzling ring designs—you'd never guess they feature lowly rhinestones (see page 106). It's proof that all that sparkles isn't genuine crystal.

The projects in this chapter range from using precision-cut crystal to incorporating ocean-tumbled glass. Despite its humble beginnings as a castaway bottle, I'll always consider sea glass a treasure. I relish the moment of discovery when you spot a piece on the beach sandwiched between pebbles, broken shells and seaweed. I've been collecting sea glass on walks for many years and have been slowly filling a bowl by our entry with my finds. I have this book to thank for making me finally turn some of that glass into jewelry (see page 114). Whether you wrap it in wire or suspend it from a drilled hole, when the light catches the glass just right, it's like that moment of discovery all over again.

CRYSTAL BALL EARRINGS

Materials

* 2 9mm x 6mm ruby Swarovski crystal ovals
* 40 (20 per ball) 4mm ruby Swarovski crystal bicones
* ruby seed beads
* 2 13" (33cm) lengths of 32-gauge beading wire
* 2 3" (8cm) lengths of .018" (5mm) stringing wire (Beadalon)
* pair of lever-back earring findings
* 2 thin silver head pins
* 4 silver crimp beads

Tools: wire cutters, round-nose pliers, chain-nose pliers

Finished length: 2" (5cm)

Swarovski packs a whole lot of sparkle into one little bead. So when you wire them together into a ball, you end up with an incredibly eye-catching earring or pendant. The best part is, it isn't as complicated as it looks. The core is a long crystal bead strung onto thin wire. Sets of three beads are strung onto the wire and wrapped around the outside of the core bead. When all is said and done, the core bead is completely concealed, and all you'll see is sparkle on all fronts.

Crystal Ball Necklace

To make this gleaming black necklace, pair round hematite beads with hematite crystals. Follow the same steps as for the earrings to make the crystal pendant, then slide it onto the center of a simple beaded strand.

ONE: Prepare to wrap first side of core bead

Thread the 32-gauge beading wire through an oval bead, pulling it through so 1" to 1¹/2" (3cm to 4cm) extends beyond the top of the bead. Thread 3 4mm bicone beads onto the long end of the wire. Bring the beaded wire up against the side of the oval bead and then thread the wire end down through the top of the bead (where the wire end extends). The beaded wire will form a loop around the oval bead, holding the beads against the outside of the bead. Pull the wire tight so the bicone beads rest against the side of the oval bead.

TWO: Continue to wrap core bead

Repeat step 1 to make 2 more beaded loops. 3 loops form half of the crystal ball.

THREE: Finish wrapping crystal

Make 3 more wraps to completely cover the core bead. Thread the beading wire up through 3 wrapped beads to bring it up next to the short wire end, twist the wires together, trim the ends and poke the twisted wire inside a bicone bead.

FOUR: Create crystal ball dangle

Thread a 4mm bicone onto the head pin, then thread the pin up through the center of the finished crystal ball, and thread on 1 more 4mm bicone. Create a wrapped loop above the beads. (See Techniques, page 140, for instructions on making a wrapped loop.)

FIVE: Link stringing wire to dangle

Thread a piece of wire through the head pin loop and bring a short tail through the loop. Thread a crimp bead onto both wires and squeeze the crimp bead flat to secure the wire.

SIX: String on beads

String 20 seed beads (or 1¹/8" [3cm]) and a crimp bead onto the wire. Bring the wire end through the opening in the earring finding, pass it back down through the crimp, and pull it tight to remove any slack. Flatten the bead with chain-nose pliers. Repeat steps 1 through 6 to create a second earring.

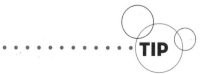

TIP

If you're having trouble locating the specified core bead, substitute an oblong glass bead. You may also use a different sized bead and adapt the number of crystals wrapped around the sides.

WOVEN EARRINGS

Materials

- 2 flower charms (Blue Moon Beads)
- matte silver, red, light pink and fuchsia Toho seed beads
- 2 long red bugle beads
- 4 4mm red round glass crystals
- 4 4mm pink round glass crystals
- 2 20" (51cm) lengths of 32-gauge silver beading wire
- ball earwires (Beadalon)
- 2 round spacers
- 2 oval jump rings

Tools: wire cutters, round-nose pliers

Finished length: 1¼" (3cm)

This beaded fabric is held together with the magic of widely available and inexpensive 32-gauge beading wire. This ultra-fine wire can easily pass multiple times through a single seed bead. The beads aren't actually woven—they're just trapped in place by two wires going through them in opposite directions. Once you're comfortable with this technique, you'll look at tiny beads in a whole new light, considering how they can be layered together to make unique earrings, pendants or rings.

Blue Woven Earrings

You can weave any kinds of small beads together to make these earrings. Remember that seven Toho seed beads equal six regular seed beads. Including bugle beads adds stability. This blue version has a total of eight rows of beads.

ONE: Bead first 2 rows

Fold the wire in half. String a red crystal, flower charm and a red crystal onto the wire, and let them drop to the folded center. Holding a wire end in each hand, string 7 fuchsia beads onto 1 end and then thread the other wire end through the same beads in the opposite direction. Pull the wire ends while carefully pushing the strung beads down to the rest over the crystals.

TWO: Bead next 2 rows

String 7 light pink seed beads through both wires and slide the row down over the fuchsia row. String a single bugle bead through both wires and slide it down so it sits over the light pink row. Bugle beads help give stability to the woven beads.

THREE: String next 3 rows

String 2 more rows of seed beads, 1 with matte silver beads and the second with fuchsia beads. String 2 pink crystals onto the wires and slide them down.

FOUR: Finish earring

Finish the woven dangle with 2 rows of light pink seed beads and a final row of red seed beads. Pass the wires back through the previous rows before trimming them. Hook a spacer through the earring finding. Pass the oval jump ring between the 2 pink rows and then hook it through the spacer before closing the jump ring. (See Techniques, page 141, for instructions on opening and closing a jump ring.)

BLING RING

Materials

* 9-hole adjustable ring
* small silver wire bead caps (Blue Moon Beads)
* large silver wire bead caps (Blue Moon Beads)
* rhinestone head pins

Tools: round-nose pliers, wire cutters

Wearing one of these bling rings puts a flash of sparkle at your fingertips that's sure to grab attention. To make this piece, string rhinestone head pins into coiled wire bead caps. Then simply hook the looped ends of the head pins around the loops of an adjustable ring base. If you're having trouble locating rhinestone head pins, you can string low-profile crystal beads onto the end of a traditional head pin instead.

⁓ Black Rhinestones

Pair rhinestone head pins with rhinestone cat's eye beads for twice the sparkle. They blend together so perfectly that they give the appearance of a manufactured setting. Experiment with different specialty head pins and beads to create original ring designs.

ONE: Thread bead caps onto head pins

Slide a small bead cap onto a head pin, so the rhinestone is nestled deep in the center of the coil. Repeat for each of the small and large bead caps.

TWO: Trim head pins

Trim the end of each head pin, leaving 3/8" (10mm) of wire beyond the bead cap.

THREE: Link dangles to ring base

Use round-nose pliers to turn a loop in each head pin wire. (See Techniques, page 140, for instructions on turning a loop.) Hook the loop into a hole on the ring. Continue adding small bead caps to each of the 9 holes.

FOUR: Add large bead caps

Add extra-large bead caps to both end loops and add 2 more to the center row. If it helps, pull open the ring to gain better access to the center row. Repeat until all the loops are filled.

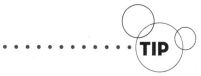

· · · · · · · · · · · ·**TIP**

Having trouble finding the bead caps used in this ring? Use wire cutters to cut coil beads in half to make two bead caps.

FLOWER VINE CHOKER

Materials

* lime green and pink seed beads
* 6 pink glass flower beads with center hole (Beadin' Path)
* 7 turquoise glass flower beads with center hole (Beadin' Path)
* 6 pink glass bud beads (Blue Moon Beads)
* 19 green glass leaf beads (Beadin' Path)
* 2 strands of satin silver stringing wire (Beadalon)
* 2 no. 2 crimp tubes
* flower toggle clasp

Tools: crimping pliers, wire cutters

Finished length: 13½" (34cm) unstretched, 18" (46cm) stretched

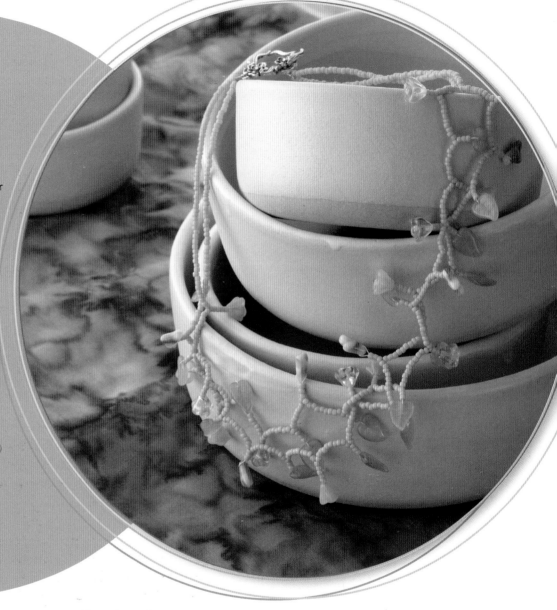

If you have flower beads in your stash, this is the perfect project for showcasing them. A simple looping of the stringing wire back through sections of your stringing creates the little leaf and flower branches off the central strand. A single strand is almost too delicate—I paired two strands to double the visual weight and make the choker more interesting.

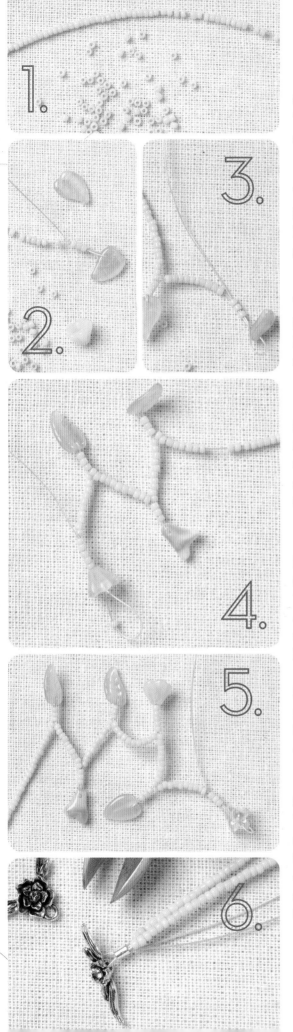

ONE: String on green seed beads

Tape 1 end of 1 strand of stringing wire and string on 3½" (9cm) of green seed beads.

TWO: String on leaf

String on 3 seeds beads and 1 leaf bead. Thread the wire back through the 3 seed beads, then string on 10 more green seed beads.

THREE: String on bud

String on 3 seed beads and a pink bud bead. Thread the wire back through the 3 seed beads, then string on 10 more green seed beads. String another leaf sequence.

FOUR: String on turquoise flower

String on 5 green beads, 1 turquoise flower bead and 1 pink seed bead. Thread the wire back down through the flower and 5 seed beads, then string on 10 more green seed beads. String another leaf sequence.

FIVE: String on pink flower

String on 3 green beads, 1 pink flower and 1 green seed bead. Thread the wire back down through the flower and through 3 seed beads, then string on 10 more seed beads. Repeat steps 2 through 5 twice, then finish with 1 more leaf sequence followed by 3½" (9cm) of seed beads.

Begin the second strand with 3½" (9cm) of green seed beads. Start with a turquoise flower sequence/leaf sequence (step 4), pink flower sequence (step 5), leaf sequence, bud/leaf sequence (step 3). Finish with 1 more turquoise flower sequence (step 4) and end with 3½" (9cm) of seed beads.

SIX: Attach clasp

Thread 1 end of each strand through a crimp tube, through 1 part of the clasp, and back through the crimp tube. Flatten the crimp tube with crimping pliers and trim away the excess wire with wire cutters. (See Techniques, page 139, for instructions on using a crimp tube.) Repeat with the other end of each strand to attach them to the other side of the clasp.

TEARDROP NECKLACE

Materials

* clear orange, tan, red, sandwashed yellow, orange and red glass teardrop beads
* pink cube beads
* red and sandwashed red E beads
* 6mm red/orange round crystals
* yellow and orange Magatama seed beads (Beadalon)
* 2 22" (56cm) lengths of 19-strand .018" (5mm) red stringing wire (Beadalon)
* 2 gold crimp tubes

Tools: wire cutters, crimping pliers

Finished length: 18¾" (48cm)

This eye-catching necklace uses two clever design devices to get your attention. The first is the unusual pairing of orange with pink, and the second is the dynamic difference in bead shape and finish: Transparent beads are strung alongside solid crystal and sandwashed beads, and organic teardrop-shaped beads contrast with spheres and cubes. It's the blending of these varied elements that makes the necklace appear complicated. You'll be amazed at how quickly and easily it strings together.

Teardrop Earrings

Stacking teardrops and turning them on their sides—is that anything like turning a frown upside down? Save a little red stringing wire, a few beads and a few crimps to whip up these earrings. Flatten a crimp at the end of a short piece of wire, then string on a few beads. Crimp the beads in place at the top of the wire with a loop and hook it to an earring finding.

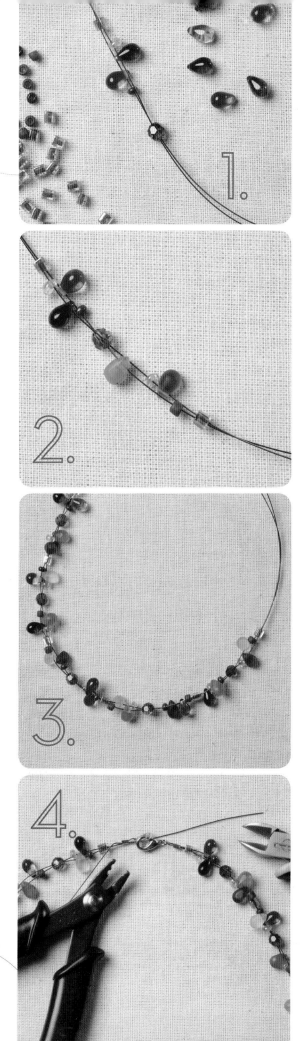

ONE: String first beaded section

Tape 1 end of both strands together. String a cube bead onto both strands. *Separate the strands and string a Magatama bead followed by a red teardrop onto 1 wire. String a tan teardrop followed by a red E bead onto the other wire. String a crystal bead onto both wires held together.

TWO: String next beaded section

Separate the strands again. String an orange sandwashed teardrop followed by a sandwashed E bead onto 1 wire. String a Magatama bead followed by a red sandwashed teardrop onto the other wire. String a cube bead onto both wires held together.

THREE: Repeat beading sequences

Repeat from * in step 1 through step 2 10 times. If necessary, adjust the spacing between the bead groupings so they're even.

FOUR: Finish necklace

Thread 1 pair of stringing wires through a crimp tube. Hook 1 of the wires through 1 side of the clasp, then bring it back down through the tube and leave the other end extending straight out of the tube. Crimp the tube flat and then fold it over. Repeat the process with the other end of the strands to connect the other side of the clasp. Trim the wires. (See Techniques, page 139, for instructions on using crimp tubes. See step 6 in the *Rolled Paper Loop Earrings*, page 84, for further visual clarification of this technique.)

FAIRY PRINCESS WINDOW PENDANT

Materials

* 1¹/₂" x 1¹/₂" (4cm x 4cm) Inkssentials memory frame (Ranger Industries)
* 2 1¹/₂" x 1¹/₂" (4cm x 4cm) Inkssentials tempered slide glass (Ranger Industries)
* butterfly sticker (Gifted Stickers Punch Studio)
* contact-sized photo image and text printed on photo paper
* 1¹/₈" x 1¹/₈" (3cm x 3cm) square of brown gold-flecked paper
* selection of glass or stone beads for dangles
* Glossy Accents glue (Ranger Industries)
* 18¹/₂" (47cm) length of suede
* 2 gold fold-over crimps
* links from brass-colored chain
* gold lobster clasp
* 2 4mm gold jump rings

Tools: scissors, chain-nose pliers, round-nose pliers

Finished length: 19" (48cm)

Photo in artwork by Donna VanDyck

I struggled over including a soldering project in this book. After a wonderful hands-on workshop with Catherine Matthews-Scanlon (www.cmscanlon.blogspot.com), I realized that it was too complex a project for me to tackle comfortably. Even though the materials are becoming more widely available, it's definitely an acquired skill, and not one I'm inclined to explore. To be honest, I still have impressive scars from my many adventures with glue guns. I specialize in "simple," so this project is my favorite alternative to soldering. Run out and find these wonderful microscope slides and frames from Ranger Ink. Both the glass and frame are so thin that the final product is truly wearable, and the best part is that there's no soldering required!

Beaded Strand

To balance the weight of the pendant, pair a chunky assortment of stone, pearl and glass beads with chain-link sections. No clasp required—the necklace is long enough to put over your head.

celia2.jpg

ONE: Cut out image and text

Cut the figure out of the background, and cut out the text of your choice.

TWO: Create collage

Apply the sticker to the brown paper square. Use Glossy Accents to glue the cut-out figure and text over the sticker.

THREE: Sandwich collage between slides

Apply more glue to the back of the brown square and sandwich it between the glass pieces. Insert the glass into the frame.

FOUR: Secure leather

Thread the metal tab through the opening and press it closed. Loop the suede through the top of the pendant. String both ends through a bent link of chain, sliding it down the suede so it rests above the loop. Use pliers to bend the link around the leather.

FIVE: Add bead dangles

String a bead onto each head pin and make a dangle with each bead, sliding the dangle onto the loop at the top of the pendant before wrapping it closed. (See Techniques, page 140, for instructions on making a wrapped loop.)

SIX: Finish necklace

Place each leather end inside a fold-over crimp. Secure the leather inside the fold-over crimps by pressing each side flat with chain-nose pliers. Hook jump rings onto the fold-over crimps and use them to connect the clasp. (See Techniques, page 141, for instructions on opening and closing a jump ring.)

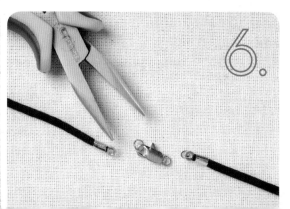

WRAPPED SEA GLASS NECKLACE

Materials

- sea glass piece
- 24-gauge silver-plated wire
- pink, blue and white tumbled glass beads
- clear tumbled glass E bead
- silver metal triangle (Blue Moon Beads)
- spring clasp
- metal ring connector (Blue Moon Beads)
- small link chain (Blue Moon Beads)
- jump rings
- head pin
- eye pins

Tools: wire cutters, chain-nose pliers, round-nose pliers

Finished length: 20" (51cm)
Finished pendant length: 2¼" (6cm) long

If you live near the coast, you might be familiar with the relaxing pastime of sea-glass hunting. While enjoying the salty air, keep your eyes peeled for glistening pieces of tumbled glass along the shoreline. Experts know hitting the beach at low tide is helpful and that a rocky shoreline increases the odds that the glass has been well tumbled. If you're landlocked, don't worry. Tumbled glass can be made or bought. Look for online instructions for tumbling glass pieces in a rock tumbler. Even easier is purchasing manufactured tumbled glass at retail outlets. It's often sold with both aquarium and flower-arranging supplies.

Wrapped Sea Glass Earrings

Wrap the glass for the earrings in a similar fashion to wrapping glass for the necklace. Simply use twin wire wraps for each one if your glass pieces are smaller, as mine are. Add bead dangles of your choice and hook your creation to an earring finding.

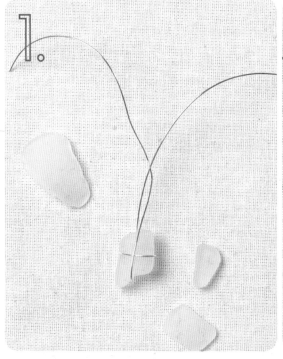

ONE: Begin wrap

Wrap the center of the wire around the middle front of the glass. Twist the wires together once at the center back of the glass (similar to tying a ribbon around a present). As you can see, sea glass comes in many different shapes and sizes. Wrap the wire around your piece of glass in the way that best secures that shape.

TWO: Secure wire wrap

Wrap 1 of the wires up around the base and front of the glass. The other wire lifts straight up against the back of the glass. Tightly twist the wires together at the top of the glass. (For demonstration purposes, I'm showing you two wrapped pieces of sea glass. The piece at left shows the back, and the piece at right shows the front.)

THREE: Create loop

Form 1 of the wires into a loop using round-nose pliers. Twist the other wire around the base of the loop to anchor it, then trim both wire ends.

There's no fixing a wire that isn't tight. If it's loose, trash the wire and start again, this time making sure your first and second twists are tight—they're the ones that hold the glass in place.

· · · · · · · · · **TIP**

Wrapping your glass pieces is a relatively quick and easy way to transform your glass pieces into jewelry. The trick is to fully and tightly trap the glass so it can't slip out. It may take you a couple of tries to get a feel for the wrapping process. No two pieces of tumbled glass are exactly alike, so if you're having trouble, switch glass pieces and try again.

FOUR: Begin to assemble pendant

Slide the eye pin up through the metal triangle, then string 3 glass beads onto the pin. Bring the pin up through the hole at the top of the triangle.

FIVE: Finish pendant

Make a wrapped loop in the head pin wire above the triangle. Trim away any excess wire. (See Techniques, page 140, for instructions on making a wrapped loop.)

SIX: Link wrapped glass to triangle

Hook the wrapped sea glass pendant onto the bottom eye pin loop.

SEVEN: Begin to assemble chain

Cut a 5" (13cm) length of chain. Hook the eye pin into the last link on the chain section. Thread 2 or 3 beads onto the pin before trimming it and use round-nose pliers to shape it into a loop. Before closing the loop and trimming the wire, hook the newly-shaped link onto a 3¼" (8cm) section of chain.

EIGHT: Finish building chain

Hook another eye pin to the end of this section, thread it with 2 or 3 beads and link it to a 4" (10cm) section of chain. Repeat the process to add a fourth 3¼" (8cm) section and a final 3" (8cm) section of chain.

NINE: Add clasp

Link a spring clasp to 1 end of the chain. Link a metal spring clasp to the other end of the chain. The spring clasp attaches to the metal ring.

TEN: Link pendant to chain

Hook the top eye pin loop of the finished pendant onto the center point of the finished chain. Carefully close the eye pin loop.

DRILLED SEA GLASS BRACELET

Materials

- found or tumbled glass
- tumbled glass beads
- clear tumbled glass E beads
- metal spacers (Beadalon)
- 10" (25cm) .015" (4mm) 49-strand stringing wire (Beadalon)
- rectangle jump rings (Beadalon)
- metal ring connector (Blue Moon Beads)
- spring clasp
- crimp beads
- plastic container
- small block of wood (needs to fit in the container)
- water

Tools: electric drill and diamond-tipped drill bit, crimping pliers, chain-nose pliers, wire cutters

Finished length: 7¹⁄₄" (18cm)

I love the look of drilled sea glass pieces, and I owe a huge thank you to my dad, Lewis Illingworth, for painstakingly drilling these pieces for me. The technique is straightforward; you need a good-quality drill, a diamond-point bit and water to keep the glass cool. Most of all you need time and patience—the process can't be rushed. Please follow all precautions to keep yourself safe.

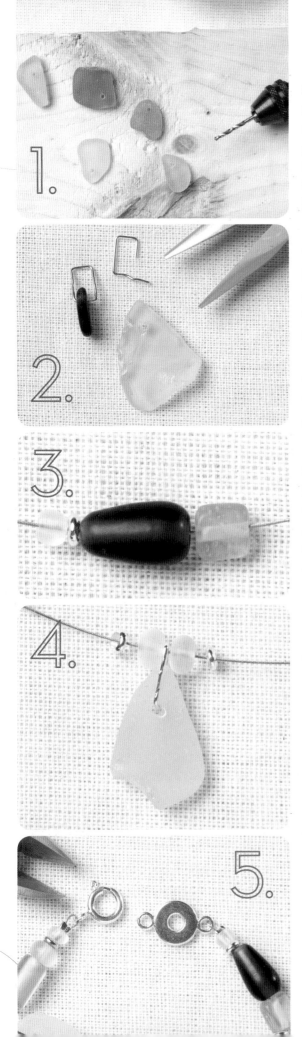

ONE: Drill glass

Place the wood in the plastic container, pour water into the container and set the glass on the wood. Splash water over the glass. Slowly drill into the glass, making sure to keep it moistened. Once you've drilled halfway through, hold it up to the light, mark the entry point on the back side of the glass and drill the other half of the hole from this side.

TWO: Slide drilled glass onto square jump rings

Fold down 1 side of a rectangle jump ring. Slide a drilled glass piece onto the wire. Use chain-nose pliers to fold the wire back up to reconnect the jump ring. Repeat the process with the other pieces of drilled glass.

THREE: Begin stringing beads

Tape the end of a piece of stringing wire and string on an E bead, a metal spacer and 1" (3cm) of random tumbled glass beads.

FOUR: Continue stringing

String the following sequence of beads: metal spacer, small tumbled glass bead, drilled glass piece, tumbled glass bead, metal spacer bead. Repeat steps 2 and 3 4 times. End with 1" (3cm) of randomly strung beads followed by a metal spacer and an E bead.

FIVE: Attach clasp

Use a crimp bead to attach a metal ring to 1 end of the bracelet and a spring clasp to the other. (See Techniques, page 138, for instructions on using crimp beads.) Trim the wires.

Drilled Sea Glass Earrings

Follow the instructions in the first step of the drilled glass bracelet to attach a rectangle-shaped jump ring to a piece of drilled glass. Add beaded dangles of your choice, then link all the pieces to earring findings.

FABRIC AND
NOTIONS

Pins and pincushions are not the only things you'll find in the sewing notions aisles. In fact, this section has become my new favorite place to hunt for jewelry-making supplies. When I spotted the button covers hanging between the fasteners and the zippers, I immediately saw their potential as jewelry elements. (You'll see them put to use as the foundation for the cast resin charms on page 60.) And the button covers are just the beginning. In this chapter, you'll find tons of projects that celebrate unexpected supplies. For example, check out the *It's-a-Snap Bracelet* (see page 126) to see how male and female snap parts joined with split rings make a super-strong bracelet base.

Buttons are the real treasures of fabric stores. They come in so many different styles, from modern to vintage and everything in between. If you're like me, it will take you awhile to narrow your selections and assemble a grouping that will work together to make a piece of jewelry. Be sure to grab a button shank remover so you can assemble the *Button Necklace* (see page 128) in this chapter.

Of course, the main attraction at any sewing store is the fabric. But who says you have to use fabric for regular old sewing projects? Pick out your favorite patterns to make the artist trading cards in this chapter (see page 136). The tiniest scrap is plenty for this project, so go ahead and assemble a wide selection of colors and patterns. It's better to be prepared—once one friend has received a card, it won't be long before you have requests for more. You should also take a look at the sequin selection at the fabric store. Check out the *Sequin Earrings* (page 124) made by sewing sequins onto loops of faux leather lace. This project turns a fanciful lightweight sewing embellishment into an integral part of the design. Also be on the lookout for wool roving supplies so you can try your hand at rolling felted beads. It's the perfect material for cold weather jewelry (see page 132).

BUCKLE BRACELET

Materials

- crystal-studded plastic buckle (Swarovski)
- 6 12" (30cm) strands of stringing elastic (Stretchmagic)
- 6 large silver crimp tubes
- turquoise and flourite beads (make sure drilled holes are large enough to accommodate stringing elastic)
- 4mm hematite Swarovski crystal bicones
- gray and metallic silver E beads

Tools: tape, chain-nose pliers, scissors

Finished length: 6" (15cm)

Simply stringing beads onto elastic is the perfect beginner beading project. Almost instantly, you're rewarded with a perfect-fitting loop of beads to slip on your wrist. In this bracelet, each strand is threaded through a buckle before being crimped in place. The buckle serves two functions: It keeps the strands together and makes a decorative focal point that frames the beaded strands.

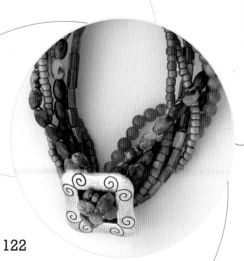

Brown Buckle Bracelet

This buckle is actually from the button aisle at a fabric store. I paired it with a neutral mix of brown and tan glass and stone beads.

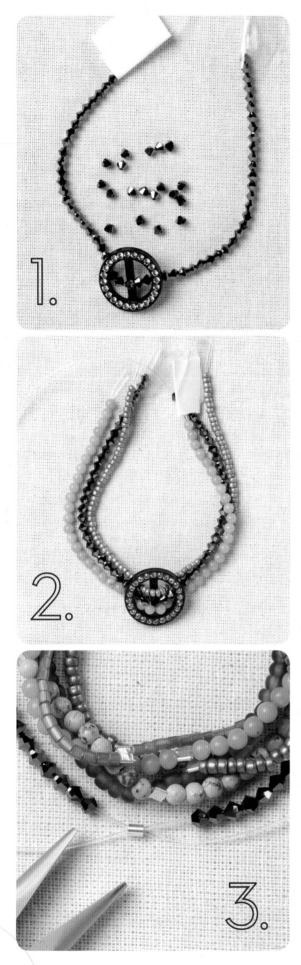

TIP

When stringing larger stone beads, it may be helpful to string four beads onto the center of the elastic, position them over the center of the buckle, then thread the elastic ends down through the sides of the buckle before stringing the remaining beads.

ONE: String first strand

Tape an end of a strand of stringing elastic and thread on 8" (20cm) of hematite crystals. Thread the beaded strand through the buckle, then tape the remaining end to temporarily secure the beads.

TWO: String remaining strands

Bead a second strand of stringing elastic with 8" (20cm) of fluorite beads, and add a third 8" (20cm) strand of silver E beads. Thread each strand through the buckle and tape the ends.

THREE: Secure strands with crimp tubes

String 3 more 8" (20cm) strands using turquoise beads, gray E beads and flourite beads. Once you've strung all 6 strands through the buckle, test fit the bracelet and make any necessary adjustments. Working with 1 strand at a time, thread the ends in opposite directions through a crimp tube, pull the strands tight and then crimp the tube flat with chain-nose" pliers. (See Techniques, page 139, for instructions on using crimp tubes.) Trim the ends of the elastic. Repeat the process for the 5 remaining strands.

TIP

Check out the scrapbooking aisle for a wide selection of buckles—you'll even find messages engraved on some of them.

SEQUIN EARRINGS

Materials

- 2 3" (8cm) lengths of pink imitation suede lace (Beadalon)
- assorted sequins, including circles and flowers
- turquoise and yellow seed beads
- pink beading thread
- earring findings
- 2 fold-over crimps
- beading needle with a hole large enough to accommodate beading thread and small enough to pass through seed beads

Tools: chain-nose pliers, scissors

Finished dangle length: 2" (5cm)

Making jewelry out of sequins is inexpensive and easy. For basically pennies a piece, you can make earrings, bracelets and necklaces. The only drawback is that when sequins stand alone, they're not terribly strong. I solved this problem by layering sequins against an imitation suede lace and anchoring them with seed bead centers.

Sequin Bracelet and Earrings

This bracelet is my favorite application of this technique—I love the shimmering long row of beads and sequins. To make your own, stitch sequins and beads onto the leather as directed for the earrings, covering the entire length of the leather strand. Use chain-nose pliers to attach a fold-over end to either end of the cord. Connect the clasp of your choice to the bracelet ends, and add a beaded dangle. Complement your bracelet with earrings made just like the pink set, but slightly shorter and with the sequins stitched onto blue leather.

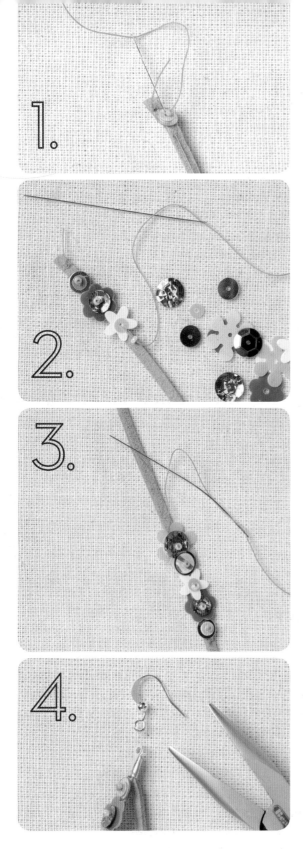

ONE: Begin to stitch on sequins and beads

Thread the beading needle, and tie a knot in the end of the beading thread. Pass the needle through the top layer of 1 of the suede pieces (this is easier than pushing the needle through the entire thickness and also hides the stitches inside the lace). If you grab the needle point with pliers, you'll get more leverage to slide it out of the leather.

Thread 2 sequins onto the needle (largest to smallest) followed by a seed bead. Thread the needle back down through the sequins. Pass the needle through the top layer of the suede under the sequin, making a small stitch and bringing the needle up where you want to place the next stack of sequins. Pull the cord taut to eliminate any slack and to keep sequins flat against the suede.

TWO: Sew on more sequins

Repeat the process to add another grouping of sequins right next to the first.

THREE: Finish sewing on sequins

Place larger sequin groups alongside smaller sequins to help visually balance your design. The larger sequins help cover the stitches between the groupings. Continue stitching sequins with bead centers until you have 4 groupings that cover half of the suede length.

FOUR: Attach leather loop to earring finding

Tie the end of the beading thread in a knot under the last sequin and trim the thread. Fold the sequined suede in half and trap the ends in a fold-over crimp. Hook the finished dangle onto the earring finding.

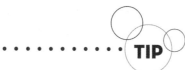

TIP

The selection of sequins is vast; a single assorted pack will offer many different sizes and colors. Be sure to check out the scrapbooking supply aisle as well. They sometimes offer a different variety of sequin products.

IT'S-A-SNAP BRACELET

Materials

* 1 package of size ¹/₁₀ sew-on snaps (10 snaps) (sold in notions department at fabric stores)
* 15 large (size 10) split rings
* 15 small (size 8) split rings (sold at fishing tackle suppliers, the jewelry variety is not strong enough)
* black and white flat circle shell beads (Blue Moon Beads)
* pearl, glass and shell bead mix (Blue Moon Beads)
* 30 head pins
* lobster clasp

Tools: wire cutters, round-nose pliers, chain-nose pliers

Finished length: 7¹/₄" (18cm)

 **TIP**

If you're having trouble manipulating the split rings, stick with the size 10 variety. The larger rings are easier to open and link together.

Link both the female and male snap parts together with sturdy split rings to make an incredibly strong bracelet base. The key is to use split rings sold with fishing tackle that are stronger than jewelry supply rings. They snap right back to their original shape after being manipulated through the metal pieces. Each snap piece has four holes. Two holes link the chain together, and the remaining two are ideal for hanging dangles. The head pin dangles feature glass, pearl and flat shell beads that are reminiscent of buttons, perfect for completing the sewing notion theme. This conversation starter is one of my everyday favorites that complements almost any outfit.

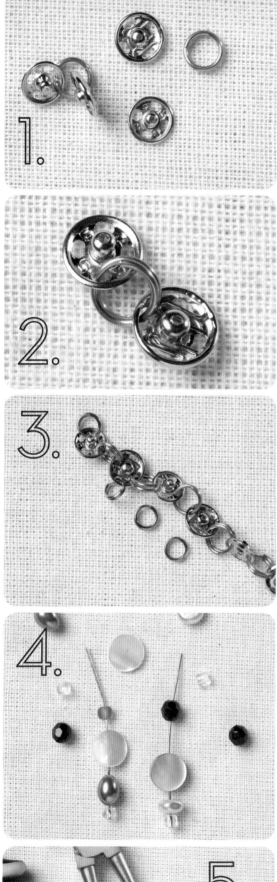

ONE: Link snaps to rings

Place the tip of the round-nose pliers into the larger size 10 split ring, a little way back from 1 of the wire ends, to temporarily pull it apart from the ring. With the tip of the round-nose pliers still held in place, thread a male and a female snap onto the separated wire end. Move the pliers out of the way.

TWO: Continue to create links

Slide the snap pieces around the ring until they're both completely connected (you've now made 1 link). Continue linking snaps and rings, alternating female with male snaps for a total of 15 snap halves and 13 size-10 split rings.

THREE: Add small split rings

Using the same round-nose pliers technique as illustrated in steps 1 and 2, add a small size 8 split ring to 1 hole in each snap part. Alternate the placement of the rings from 1 side to another with each snap part.

FOUR: Create beaded dangles

String 2 head pins with an assortment of E beads and pearls from the bead mix, positioning a flat shell bead in the center of the beads. Make a loop above each bead with round-nose pliers. (See Techniques, page 140, for instructions on turning a loop.)

FIVE: Link dangles to chain

Thread both dangles through 1 of the size 8 rings before wrapping the loops closed and trimming away the excess wire. (See Techniques, page 140, for instructions on making a wrapped loop.) Repeat the process to add 2 dangles to each of the size 8 rings for a total of 30 dangles.

SIX: Finish bracelet

Use a size 10 ring to attach a lobster clasp to 1 end of the finished bracelet and add the last ring to the other end of the bracelet.

BUTTON NECKLACE

Materials

* white and black plastic buttons with shanks (La Mode, Blumenthal Lansing)
* flat, round and rectangular black faceted glass beads (Blue Moon Beads)
* 4mm, 6mm and 8mm glass pearls (CCA)
* 6mm and 8mm pink Swarovksi crystal rounds
* 21" (53cm) and 24" (61cm) lengths of .018" (5mm) black stringing wire (Beadalon)
* black crimp beads
* 2-piece 12mm floral clasp (CCA)
* Aleene's platinum glass and bead glue
* crimp tube

Tools: button shank remover, crimping pliers, wire cutters

Finished length: 23" (58cm)

I love the vintage appearance of these black and white plastic buttons. By simply clipping off the backs of the buttons with a shank remover, you've transformed the button into a flat cabochon. Glue a pair of buttons back to back, trapping the stringing wire in between them to make a bead. If you don't have the time to string a whole necklace, consider gluing single button fronts to earring posts to make instant earrings.

ONE: Prepare buttons

To remove the plastic shanks from the backs of the buttons, position the clipper blades flush with the back of the button to remove as much plastic as possible. You'll need 2 same-sized flat-backed buttons to make each button bead.

TWO: String necklace

Tape the end of the 21" (53cm) wire strand and string on the following sequence of beads: 8mm pink crystal bead, crimp bead, black faceted rectangle bead, crimp bead, 6mm pink crystal bead, 6mm pearl, 4mm pearl, black crimp bead, round black faceted bead, crimp bead, 4mm pearl, 8mm pearl, crimp bead, black faceted bead, crimp bead.

THREE: Crimp beads in place

Spread the beads out along the strand, leaving spaces to add the button beads. Using the crimping pliers or chain-nose pliers, flatten the crimp beads on either side of the black faceted beads to hold them in place.

FOUR: Add button beads

Lay the paired buttons from step 1 along the strand in their intended positions. Apply glue to the back sides of 1 white button and 1 black and sandwich the stringing wire between the pair. Repeat the process to assemble button beads directly to the strand. Turn the beads so they're flat and let them dry undisturbed.

FIVE: Add clasp

Repeat steps 1 through 4 with the 24" (61cm) strand, substituting the following beading sequence: crimp bead, round black faceted bead, crimp bead, 6mm pink crystal bead, 8mm pearl, 4mm pearl, crimp bead, black faceted rectangle, crimp bead, 8mm pink crystal bead, 4mm pearl, crimp bead, round black faceted bead, crimp bead. After the button beads have dried, secure 1 end of both wires to 1 clasp component with a crimp tube (See Techniques, page 139, for instructions on using a crimp tube.) Repeat to attach the strand ends to the other half of the clasp.

LEATHER BRACELET

Materials

- 24" (61cm) brown leather cord
- 36" (91cm) brown waxed linen cord (Blue Moon Beads)
- 6mm vintage round opal Lucite beads (Beadin' Path), or choose any low-profile bead with a hole large enough to accommodate a double thickness of the waxed linen
- flat 2-hole silver button (La Mode, Blumenthal)
- fish charm (Blue Moon Beads)

Tools: scissors

Finished length: 7 3/4" (20cm)

Smooth leather cord easily folds and knots into this comfortable cuff. Waxed cord grips the leather and weaves in and out of the beads to suspend them between the leather cords. The silver metal button and charm are not just decorative—they help secure the knot-and-loop closure.

Moonglow Bracelet

Experiment with different beads and buttons. This variation features grey moonglow oblong beads and an ornate button. Skip the charm for a streamlined look.

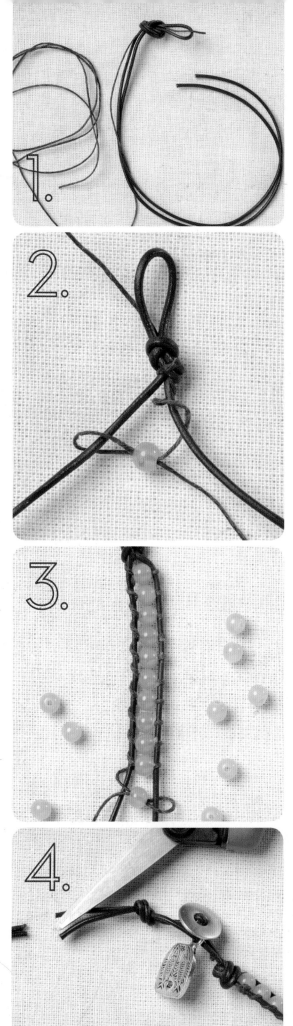

ONE: Knot leather cord and waxed linen
Fold the leather in half, hold the fold and one end of the wax cord together and tie them in an overhand knot. The knotted loop serves 2 functions: It becomes half of the closure and anchors the waxed linen to the bracelet.

TWO: Wrap first bead in place
Tightly wrap the waxed linen twice around the top leather cord, positioning the wraps directly alongside the overhand knot. * Thread a bead onto the linen, then wrap the linen around the bottom leather cord. Thread the linen end back up through the bead again, then wrap the cord once around the top cord.

THREE: Continue wrapping beads in place
Repeat the process from the * in step 2 until you have 5³/4" (15cm) of beads between the cords.

FOUR: Finish bracelet
Tie all 3 cords into an overhand knot, and trim off the waxed linen. Thread the button onto 1 cord and the charm onto the other. Tie the leather cords in a final overhand knot to trap the button and charm in place. Trim the leather ends 1" (3cm) from the knot.

FELTED BEADS NECKLACE

Materials

* teal, brown and purple wool roving (found at yarn, spinning and weaving suppliers)
* assorted silver metal bead caps (Blue Moon Beads)
* purple foil, opaque and clear turquoise and beige E beads
* 6mm blue miracle beads
* 4mm purple miracle beads
* 6mm brown and dark brown round wood beads (Blue Moon Beads)
* brown and turquoise rectangle glass beadlettes
* 1 glass flower bead
* 20" (51cm) .018" (5mm) stringing wire (Beadalon)
* rectangle toggle clasp (Blue Moon Beads)
* 2 crimp beads
* small sewing needle with hole large enough to accommodate stringing wire
* dish soap
* warm water
* bubble wrap

Tools: crimping pliers, wire cutters

Finished length: 17¼" (44cm)
Finished felt beads: ½" (1cm)

I love crafty mornings with a friend and a good cup of coffee. I owe my friend Hannah Beattie another thank you for bringing over her wool roving collection and teaching me how to make these nifty beads. I was hooked the moment the sudsy fibers tightened and formed a bead in my finger-tips. The design dilemma was finding a way to turn these little balls into wearable jewelry. Framing them with bead caps and balancing them with miracle and wood beads turned out to be the perfect solution. I'm looking forward to bringing these pieces out next fall and enjoying them through the cold winter months.

ONE: Shape roving into ball

Pull off some roving, and use your fingertips to wrap it into a small ball, adding sections of roving to enlarge the ball. Switch directions when you add a new section of roving.

TWO: Begin to felt ball

Fill a small basin with warm water and add just a few drops of soap. Use your fingertips to dampen the ball with the warm water. Squeeze a tiny drop of soap into the palm of your hand and lightly roll the ball in your palm to cover it with the soap. Squeeze and rotate the ball to agitate the fibers and felt them together. Periodically check the surface of the bead. If the fibers are clumping together and causing a break in the bead, try these tips to correct the situation: Pull the clumped fibers apart and stretch them over the surface of the bead, add a new layer of roving around the bead and dampen it, or rub the clumped fibers against bubble wrap to help them fuse with the fibers around them.

THREE: Finish felting ball

The ball will end up reducing by 1/3 to 1/2 its original size during the felting process. (The bead on the left is not yet fully felted, while the bead on the right is completely compressed.) Once the surface of your bead is well integrated, apply more pressure and roll it between the palms of your hand, adding more water if necessary. You'll soon feel the bead shrinking and hardening. Let it dry completely before stringing.

FOUR: Begin stringing necklace

Thread on 3 1/4" (6cm) random assortment of E beads, miracle beads, wood beads and beadlettes.

FIVE: String on felt beads

String on the bead cap, then thread the needle onto the stringing wire and push the needle through a felt bead (use chain-nose pliers to help pull the needle out), then remove the needle and string on the second bead cap. String on 1⅓" (3cm) of random beads.

SIX: Attach clasp

Repeat step 5 4 times. Add 2⅔" (7cm) of beads before adding the clasp to either end with a crimp bead. (See Techniques, page 138, for instructions on using a crimp bead.)

Felt Bead Earrings

Felt a matching pair of beads in your favorite colors to make these dangle earings. Save pairs of ornate bead caps and beads to frame your handiwork.

Prayer Box Necklace

Surprisingly, this necklace only uses two felt beads.
I enjoyed the process of embellishing the large bead
with seed beads. Both its size and sparkle are the perfect
counterbalance to the heavy prayer box charm.

Assemble the center dangle with a 6" (15cm) length of stringing wire,
just as for the earring, except begin and end by looping
the stringing wire through 2 6mm decorative jump rings.
Between the rings, string on: small plain bead cap, 1/3" (1cm)
brown felt bead, small plain bead cap, large ornate bead
cap, 1/2" (2cm) orange felt bead, large ornate bead cap,
ornate spacer. Use a needle and orange thread to sew seed
beads all over the orange bead. Link the prayer box to the
jump ring at the end of the dangle.

String the 19" (48cm) length of stringing wire with 8¹/4"
(21cm) of random beads, add the finished dangle and then
string on 8¹/4" (21cm) of random beads. Attach a clasp.

Materials

* 1/3" (1cm) brown felt beads
* 1/2" (2cm) orange felt bead
* prayer box charm (Blue Moon Beads)
* 2 pairs of bead caps, 1 small plain and 1 large and ornate
* 1 ornate spacer bead
* 4mm green miracle beads
* 6mm turquoise and brown miracle beads
* 6mm brown and dark brown wood beads
* 6mm turquoise bicone and round crystals
* metallic brown, chartreuse green, clear orange and opaque red E beads
* green, brown and tan seed beads
* 1 19" (48cm) and 1 6" (15cm) length of stringing wire (Beadalon)
* O-ring and toggle clasp (Blue Moon Beads)
* 6mm plain silver jump ring
* 2 6mm decorative jump rings
* 2 medium crimp beads
* orange sewing thread
* small sewing needle with hole large enough to accommodate stringing wire

Tools: chain-nose pliers, crimping pliers, wire cutters

Finished length: 17¹/4" (44cm)

FABRIC-AND-BEAD ARTIST TRADING CARD

Materials

* turquoise and black-and-white patterned cotton fabric scraps
* blue tulle
* playing card (from a regular deck)
* white cotton/flannel cloth scrap for a backing
* sequins
* clear foil E beads
* black Magatama beads
* silver metal star charm
* fabric-covered letter brads
* straight pins
* Aleene's platinum bond fabric glue
* orange and blue sewing thread
* sewing machine outfitted with a heavy needle for stitching through the card and fabric layers

Tools: wire cutters, chain-nose pliers, scissors

Finished size: 3¹/₂" (9cm) x 2¹/₂" (6cm)

It's appropriate that I made this project with my creative friend Hannah Beattie. She's a whiz at art quilts, and she converted one of her quilting techniques to work as a trading card/decorative hanging. I had the fun job of embellishing the beautiful fabric-covered cards with beads and scrapbook embellishments.

Another ATC

Use your imagination and any fabric and beading materials you have on hand to make more ATCs. This version has an eyelet that doubles as a decorative hanging.

ONE: Cut, layer and pin fabric in place
Make your design by laying strips of black-and-white fabric over the turquoise fabric. Place the scrap of white fabric under the arrangement and a layer of tulle over it. Pin the stack to hold the pieces in place.

TWO: Stitch layered fabric together
With your machine threaded with orange thread, stitch 3 horizontal and 3 vertical seams to hold the stacked fabric together.

THREE: Stitch fabric to card
Invert the fabric and place the card over the center of the fabric. Stitch 2 vertical and 2 horizontal seams through the card and the fabric. Use the zigzag setting to stitch around the edge of the card. Trim the excess fabric off the edges.

FOUR: Embellish card
Use wire cutters to cut the metal tabs off the backs of the brads. Glue them directly to the front (fabric side) of the card, and let them set. Thread a sewing needle with blue thread and stitch turquoise sequins with black bead centers, crystal beads and the charm around the letters. Pass the needle between the fabric and card so you can't see the stitches between the embellishments. If it helps, grab the needle with chain-nose pliers to pull the needle through the fabric. Enter and exit the card from the outside edge. The zigzag stitch will help camouflage your knots.

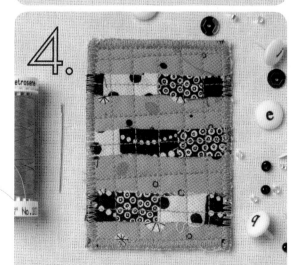

TIP

Try miniaturizing this project to make earrings and pendants. Just follow the steps using a small section of card as your base and substitute small eyelets and embellishments.

TECHNIQUES

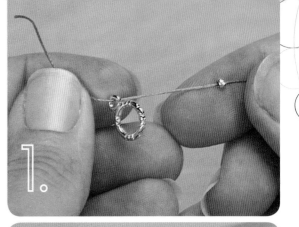

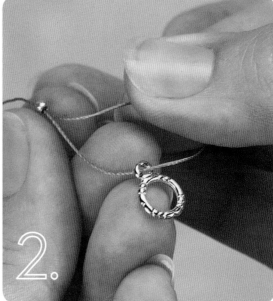

Despite the tremendous variety in finished beaded jewelry pieces, most share the same basic techniques. Take a little time to familiarize yourself with these simple processes—especially how to shape head pins and how to secure clasps to the ends of beaded strands with crimp tubes and beads. Once you're comfortable with the steps, you'll find assembling the actual projects very simple. Any special techniques will be fully explained in each project.

Using Crimp Beads

The crimp bead is sized between a small crimp tube and a standard crimp tube. It's not as secure as the standard crimp tube because it can only be crimped a single time. Use crimp beads to attach clasps onto lighter-weight beading cord and to station beads on stringing wire.

ONE: String crimp and clasp onto wire or cord
String 1 crimp bead followed by 1 part of the clasp onto the beading cord. Position them about ½" to 1" (1cm to 3cm) from the wire end.

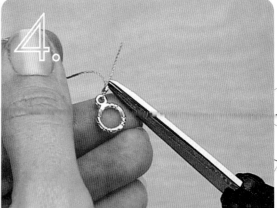

TWO: Thread cord or wire back through bead
Thread the end back through the crimp bead, and then pull the end to tighten the loop with the clasp. Make sure the crimp bead is positioned exactly where you want it.

THREE: Flatten crimp
Clamp the crimping pliers onto either side of the crimp bead. Squeeze the pliers to trap the double thickness of cord or wire inside the flattened bead. You may also use chain-nose pliers to flatten crimp beads.

FOUR: Trim away excess cord or wire
Separate the cords where they emerge from the bead, and then carefully cut off the remaining cord end. Use scissors to cut cord and wire cutters to trim wire.

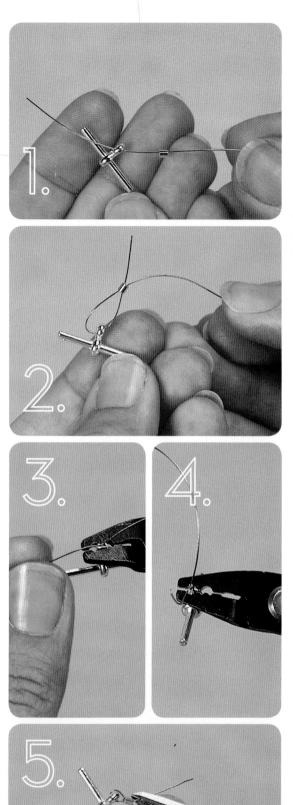

Using Crimp Tubes

Use this double-crimp technique when using no. 2 crimp tubes or larger. A single crimp will anchor the clasp to the strand, but the second fold makes the connection even stronger. It also serves to narrow the crimp so it blends into the finished piece.

ONE: String on crimp tube and clasp

String 1 crimp tube followed by 1 part of the clasp onto the end of a wire strand. Position them about 1/2" to 1" (1cm to 3cm) from the end of the wire.

TWO: Thread the strand back through crimp

Fold the strand end back through the crimp tube. Pull the end to tighten the loop with the clasp.

THREE: Flatten crimp

Separate the wires inside the crimp tube so they rest against opposite sides of the tube (wires should not cross inside the tube). Clamp the crimping pliers over the outside of the tube, aligning the bumps in the tool with the center of the tube. Squeeze the crimping tool to flatten the tube's center and simultaneously trap the strings on the sides.

FOUR: Fold crimp in half

Use 1 of the rounded openings in the crimping tool to bring the sides of the tube together, essentially folding the flattened tube in half.

FIVE: Trim away excess wire

Separate the strands where they emerge from the crimp tube, and then carefully cut off the remaining wire end flush with the edge of the crimp tube. Use scissors to cut cord and wire cutters to trim wire.

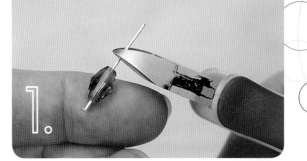

Turning a Loop in a Head Pin

This technique transforms any bead into a charm or dangle. It is quick and easy to turn the wire end into a loop. The only drawback is that if the loop is pulled, it can come apart and fall off the jewelry. If you're placing the dangle where it might get caught or pulled, substitute the wrapped loop technique.

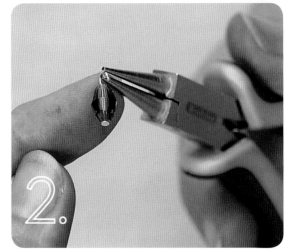

ONE: Cut head pin wire

Slide a bead onto a head pin. Use wire cutters to cut the head pin wire to about 1/2" (13mm) above the bead. For larger beads, cut the wire to about 3/8" (1cm).

TWO: Create loop

Grab the head pin wire near the end with round-nose pliers and twist the pliers toward yourself to create a loop. Use round-nose and chain-nose pliers to make fine adjustments to secure the loop.

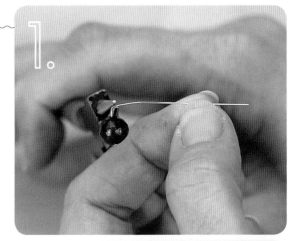

Making a Wrapped Loop

A wrapped loop is the strongest way to finish a head pin, and it's the preferred way to make earrings. Don't skimp when buying head pins, especially when you're learning this technique. Sterling head pin wires are so flexible you can almost wrap them with your fingertips. Wait until you're comfortable before using decorative head pins. They're made of layered metals that make them harder to manipulate.

ONE: Bend wire above bead

Slide a bead onto a head pin and grab the wire above the bead with round-nose pliers. Bend the wire over the pincer at a 90 degree angle.

TWO: Create loop in wire

Wrap the wire completely around the nose of the round-nose pliers to create a loop.

THREE: Wrap loop

Hold the loop with the round-nose pliers and use your fingers or chain-nose pliers to wrap the tail end of the wire around the base of the loop several times. Trim away excess wire with wire cutters.

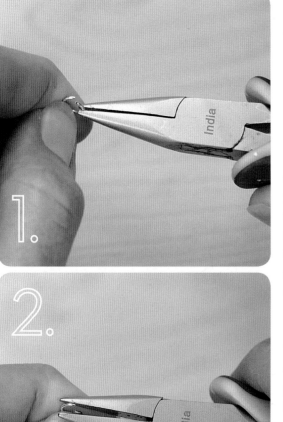

Opening and Closing a Jump Ring

Jump rings are handy connectors. You can use them to extend a finished piece before adding a clasp, or to join a short length of chain to one end of a necklace or bracelet. The trick is to open and close jump rings laterally so they keep their shape.

ONE: Grab jump ring at break

Hold 1 side of the jump ring between your thumb and index finger, just below the break in the metal. Grab the other side of the jump ring with your fingers or with chain-nose pliers and pull the wire toward you to open it. Be careful not to open the jump ring by pulling the wire ends away from each other, as horizontal action can distort the shape of the jump ring and weaken it.

TWO: Close jump ring

Close the jump ring by sandwiching the wires between the pincers of the chain-nose pliers. Apply even pressure to bring the wire ends firmly back together.

RESOURCES

The projects in this book call for a wide range of different materials. Everything you need is readily available from craft and hobby stores, hardware stores, yarn and fiber shops, fishing tackle suppliers and local discount department stores. If you have trouble finding a particular product used in the book, consult the list of manufacturers below. Visit their Web sites to find out where their products are sold near you.

Beadalon
www.beadalon.com
beading tools, stringing wires, faux lace, rubber tubing, findings, Bead Fix Glue, spacers, Magatama beads, wire guardians, watch faces, silver-plated wire

Blue Moon Beads
www.creativityinc.com
glass, stone, shell, wood and ceramic beads, link chain and findings in different metal finishes, charms, metal disks and game pieces

Blumenthal Lansing Company
www.buttonsplus.com
La Mode buttons

Cousin Corporation of America (CCA)
www.cousin.com
glass pearls, clasp

CRYSTALLIZED Swarovski Elements
www.create-your-style.com
machine-cut Swarovski crystal beads

DecoArt
www.decoart.com
Triple Thick Glaze, Liquid Beadz Glue

Delta Creative Inc.
www.deltacreative.com
acrylic paints

Duncan
www.duncancrafts.com
E 6000, Aleene's Platinum Bond Glass and Bead Glue, Aleene's Platinum Bond Fabric Glue

Envirotex
www.eti-usa.com
cast resin solution

Fiskars
www.fiskars.com
paper trimmer, clear stamps, soft-touch scissors

Grafix
www.grafixarts.com
shrink art sheets

Making Memories
www.makingmemories.com
instant setter

Ranger Industries Inc.
www.rangerink.com
Glossy Accents, slide glass and frames

Sculpey Clay
www.sculpey.com
Sculpey, Premo, Ultralight polymer clays

The Beadin' Path
www.beadinpath.com
vintage beads, silk cord, center-drilled charms, Lucite beads

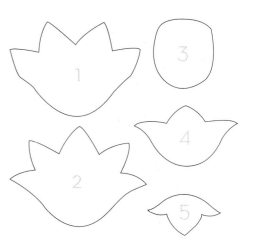

Enlarge templates for Paper Petal Pin, top, and Brown and Pink Pin, bottom, (page 86) by 159%.

INDEX

FIND INSPIRATION AND INSTRUCTION
for Making Even More Beautiful Jewelry in These North Light Books

SIMPLY BEAUTIFUL BEADED JEWELRY
by Heidi Boyd

Author and designer Heidi Boyd has filled this fabulous jewelry book to the brim with over 50 gorgeous beaded necklaces, bracelets, earrings and accessories. Her trademark style shines in each of the projects and variations. Best of all, every piece is simple to make and beautiful to wear. Even a beginning crafter can easily finish any project in the book in one afternoon. The book includes a helpful techniques section and insightful tips scattered throughout.

ISBN 13: 978-1-58180-774-5
ISBN-10: 1-58180-774-0
paperback, 128 pages, 33445

PLEXI CLASS
by Tonia Davenport

Discover a modern, industrial twist on mixed-media art jewelry. *Plexi Class* features 30 cutting-edge projects that all start with plastic, such as Plexiglas, vinyl or shrink plastic. In addition to learning how to cut Plexiglas, you'll also learn how to shape it into earrings, charms and pendants, and you'll see how easy it is to combine plastic with your favorite papers, embellishments and other mixed-media materials.

ISBN-13: 978-1-60061-061-5
ISBN-10: 1-60061-061-7
paperback, 128 pages, Z1753

PERFECT MATCH
by Sara Schwittek

Perfect Match is filled to the brim with 40 plus fabulous earring designs for all occasions. From a day on the beach to a night out on the town, you will learn how to make earrings to go with every outfit and outing. Sara Schwittek will teach you all about the tools and

techniques used to make her fabulous earring designs in as little as 15 minutes. From simple dangles to sophisticated chandeliers, you are sure to find your perfect match!

ISBN-13: 978-1-60061-068-4
ISBN-10: 1-60061-068-4
paperback, 160 pages, Z1803

PRETTY LITTLE FELTS
by Julie Collings

Inside this playful book, you'll find more than 30 projects to tickle your fancy. *Pretty Little Felts* shows you how to combine all kinds of felt with unexpected mixed-media materials, including vintage fabric, paper, glitter, metal, beads, ribbon and wire. From useful pouches and needle books to delicate jewelry and whimsical ornaments and doodads, there's something

here for every crafter. All the projects are simply made with basic sewing and papercrafting techniques. A helpful getting started section gives information on dyeing and stitching felt, as well as specific instructions on deconstructing wool clothing.

ISBN-13: 978-1-60061-090-5
ISBN-10: 1-60061-090-0
pages, Z1979

These and other fine North Light Books are available at your local craft retailer, bookstore or online supplier, or visit our Web site at www.mycraftivity.com.